The New Book of CHINESE LATTICE DESIGNS

by Daniel Sheets Dye

Edited and with an Introduction by
Nancy Balderston Conrad

DOVER PUBLICATIONS, INC., NEW YORK

DANIEL SHEETS DYE WISHED
THAT THIS VOLUME BE DEDICATED TO
THE MEMORY OF HIS WIFE
JANE BALDERSTON DYE
AND TO THEIR MANY NIECES AND NEPHEWS

Published in Canada by General Publishing Company, Ltd., 30 Lesmill Road, Don Mills, Toronto, Ontario.
Published in the United Kingdom by Constable and Company, Ltd., 10 Orange Street, London WC2H 7EG.

The New Book of Chinese Lattice Designs is a new work, first published by Dover Publications, Inc., in 1981.

DOVER *Pictorial Archive* SERIES

The New Book of Chinese Lattice Designs belongs to the Dover Pictorial Archive Series. Up to ten illustrations from it may be used in any single publication without payment to or permission from the publisher. Wherever possible include a credit line, indicating title, author and publisher. Please address the publisher for permission to make more extensive use of illustrations in this volume than that authorized above.
The reproduction of this book in whole is prohibited.

International Standard Book Number: 0-486-24128-9
Library of Congress Catalog Card Number: 81-65377

Manufactured in the United States of America
Dover Publications, Inc.
180 Varick Street
New York, N.Y. 10014

INTRODUCTION

by
Nancy Balderston Conrad

In 1974 Dover Publications, Inc., reprinted Daniel Sheets Dye's *Chinese Lattice Designs,* a work which had first appeared in 1937 as *A Grammar of Chinese Lattice* and which has been regarded as the definitive work on the subject ever since. It contained over 1200 designs arranged according to the system of classification devised by Dr. Dye himself. But only a portion of Dr. Dye's enormous collection could be reproduced in that volume for the simple reason of space. The lattice designs presented in the present volume were chosen from those which, although not included in the first volume, were in no way inferior. Also included are some of the designs drawn between 1937 and 1949, when Dr. Dye retired after 40 years in China. For a full description of the history, construction and classification of the lattice, the reader can do no better than refer to Dr. Dye's text in *Chinese Lattice Designs* (Dover 23096-1).

Lattice windows, which have been used in China for at least 3,000 years, began to give way to glass soon after Dr. Dye arrived at Chengtu in 1908 to teach science at the then-forming West China Union University. Many of the old windows were destroyed in the series of revolutions and local wars that took place from 1911 to 1949. These windows, with paper pasted on them to keep out the winter winds, were such everyday items that the Chinese did not regard them as worth cataloging. This volume adds to the collection of designs that have been preserved. The majority of the patterns were collected in Szechwan Province, West China, and in the city of Chengtu in particular. Chengtu had for centuries been a trade center and many of the windows there showed foreign influences. When Dr. Dye first came there, it was virtually untouched by modern Western influences. Professors at Dr. Dye's alma mater, Denison, and at the University of Wisconsin advised him to have a hobby which would fill his leisure time and lessen the cultural shock and homesickness which they knew a young man from Ohio farm country would experience.

After retirement, Dr. Dye and his wife Jane spent ten years as host and hostess at the John Woolman Memorial in Mt. Holly, New Jersey, and then moved to Colora, Maryland, where they continued their literary interests and research. Before her death on November 26, 1976, Jane Dye published a small volume on the birds of West China. Daniel Dye continued his work on lattice, Chiang belt patterns, the origin of the swastika, and Kansu mortuary pottery until the last weeks of his life. He died on September 9, 1977, in his ninety-third year.

Daniel Sheets Dye

Yang Chi-shang

PREFACE

by
Daniel Sheets Dye

On Chinese New Year's Day, 1916, while teaching at the West China Union University, I spied some striking lattice windows at the famous Ts'ao T'ang Ssu erected in honor of the T'ang dynasty poet Tu Fu. I collected twenty specimens of the designs, not realizing that this would become a major occupation.

The windows were unevenly lighted, so photographing them with the equipment available at the time was an impossibility. Nor did I have time time to make detailed drawings, for compelling teaching duties and other commitments called for more time than I had at my disposal.

I had a series of personal teacher-secretaries who taught us Chinese and wrote our letters. Some drew our teaching charts and wrote out examination papers so that each student could have a copy. For several hours each day they had nothing to do but wait until we were out of class. Finally I found a teacher, Mr. Yang Chi-shang, to whom I could teach the use of my mechanical drawing instruments.

My study was in an old farmhouse. The main part of the house had been refurbished with wooden floors and glass windows, but the back portion had the more customary earthen floors and lattice windows. We went into the back, and Teacher Yang watched me measure and draw the lattice window. He worked for weeks until he had mastered the technique. The drawings presented in this volume would not have been made if Teacher Yang had not done such meticulous work over the years until his death in 1936. When you appreciate these drawings, remember Teacher Yang!

I collected the designs on the road, for I had more sedan-chair travel than the reader can imagine a full-time teacher could have between 1908 and 1949. I would get out of my "chair," measure and sketch a window that caught my eye, and catch up with the caravan at the next rest stop. I brought measurements, sketches and sometimes chalk rubbings from all over West China to Teacher Yang, who turned them into drawings. How were they to be rendered? Should we blacken the frame alone, the inner frame alone, the uncut vertical bar, or the cut crossbars, or should we blacken all frames and bars? I felt that this was too much and would give a false impression of lattice, which never looks so black or white. We finally decided to detail the drawings as you find them done in most of the plates—in double thin lines—and let the details speak for themselves.

CONTENTS

The contents of this volume follow the system of classification established by Dr. Dye in *Chinese Lattice Designs.*

IV. LINE ENDING.

V. BROKEN LINE.

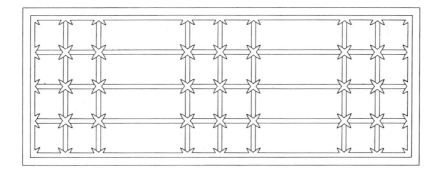

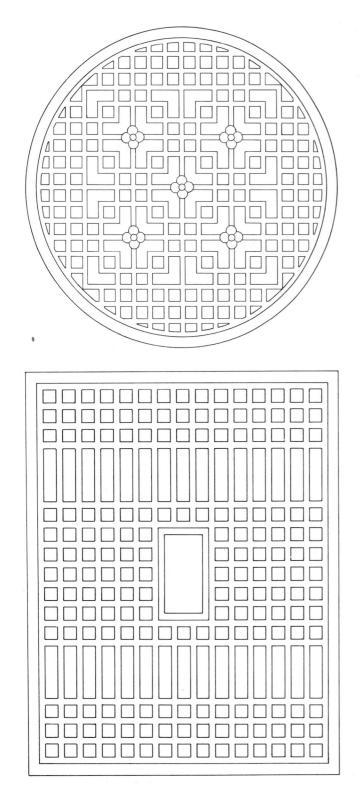

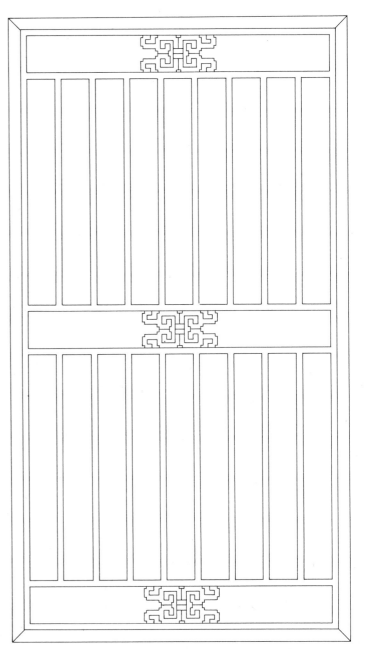

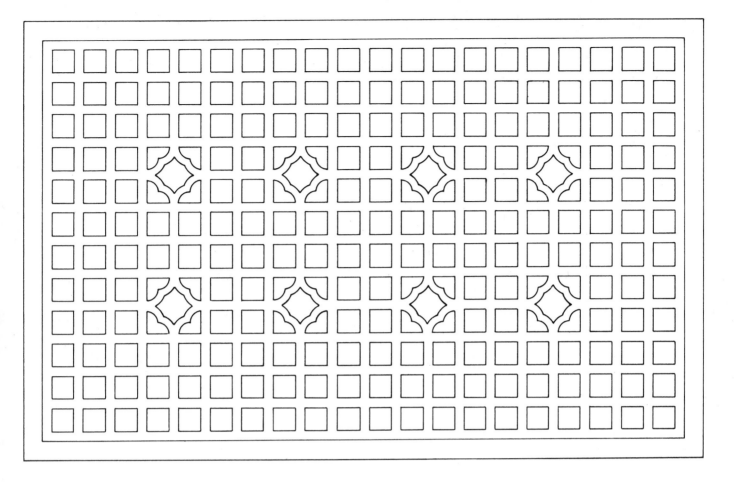

8 Octagon

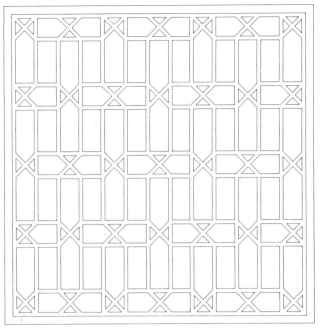

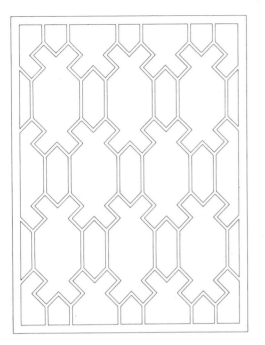

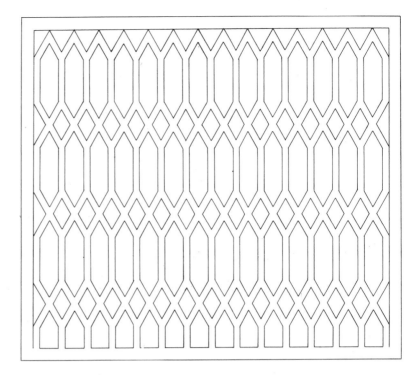

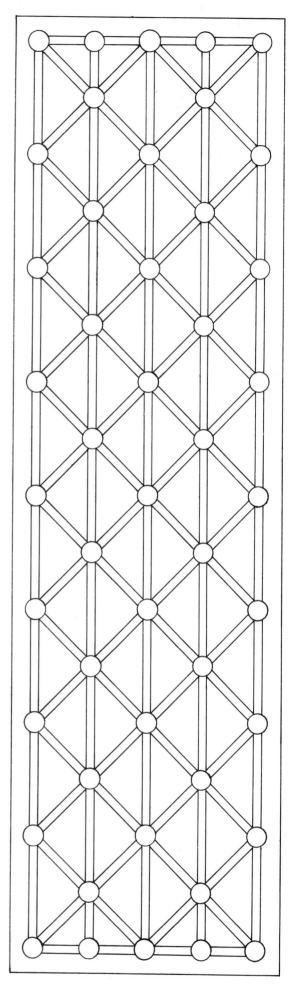

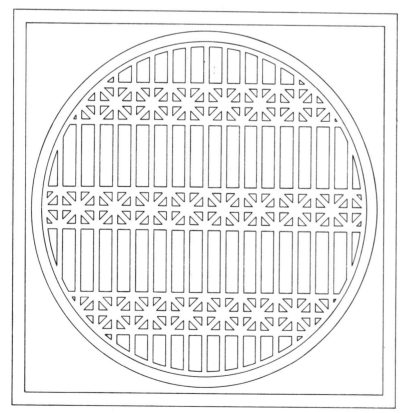

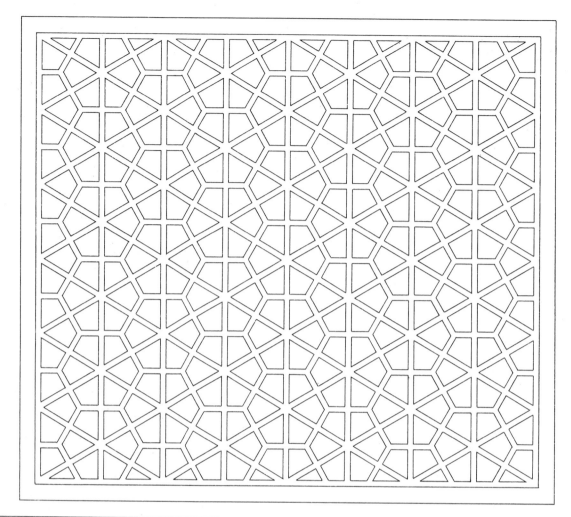

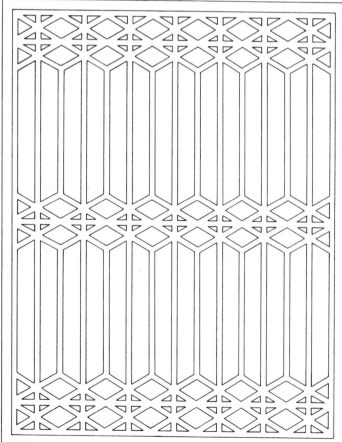

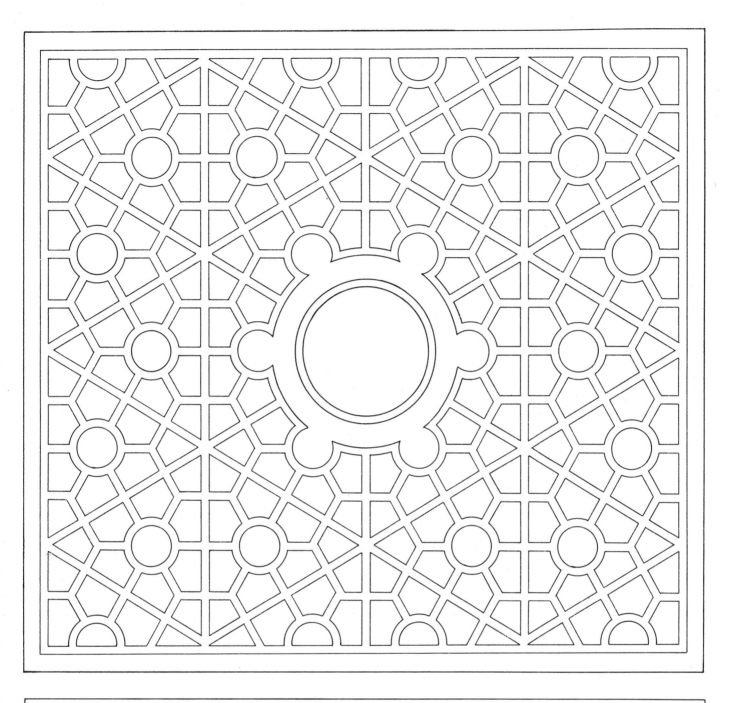

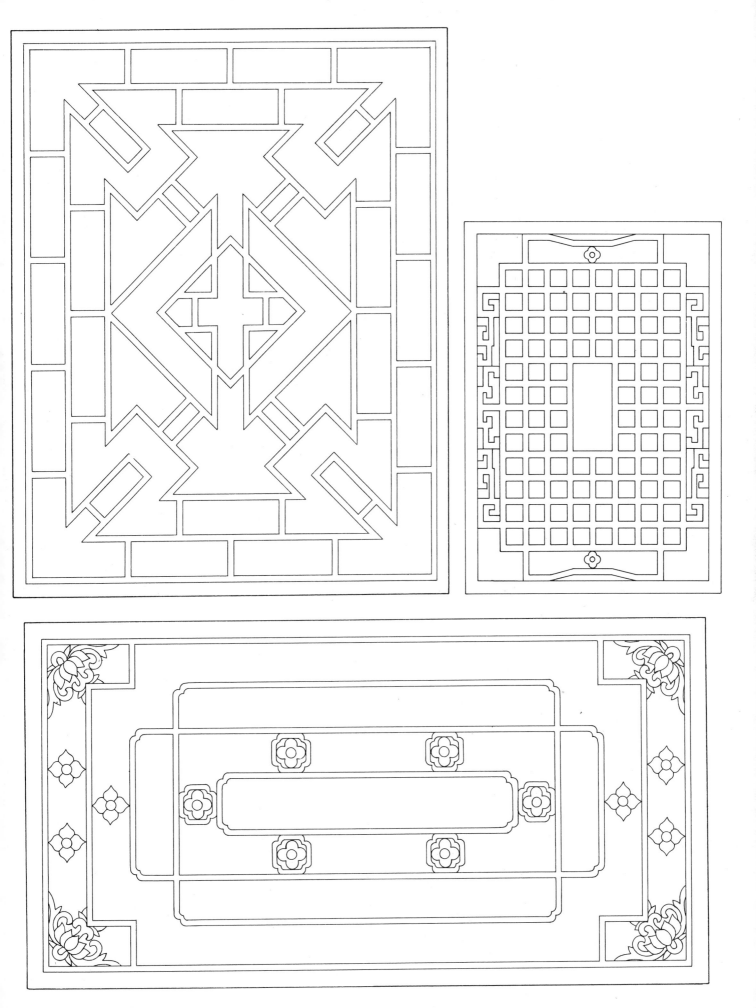

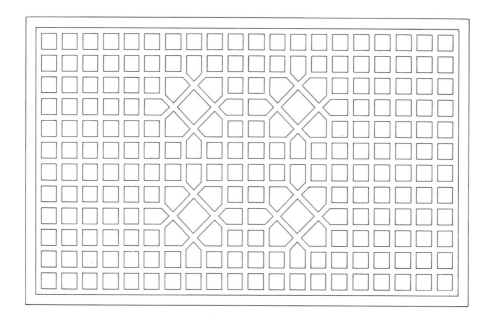

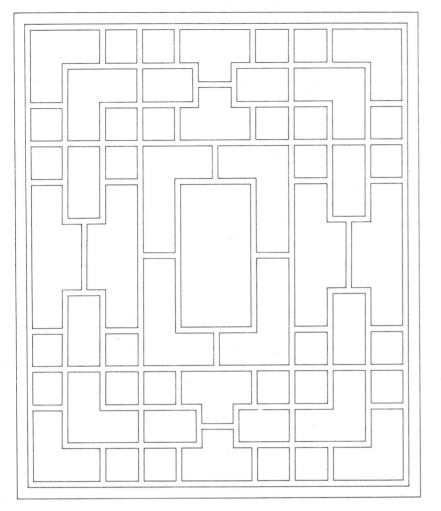

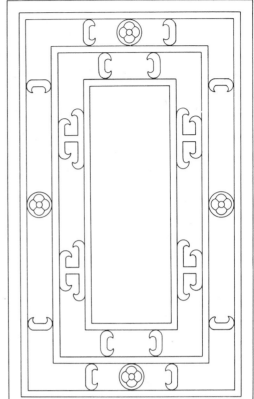

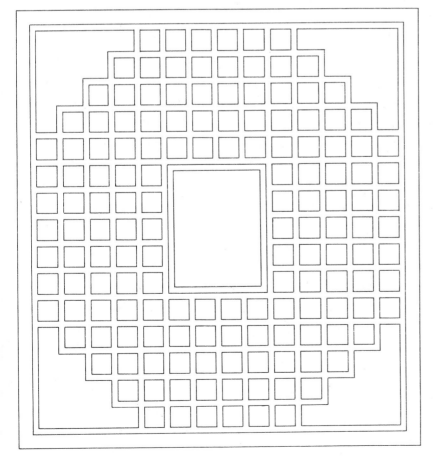

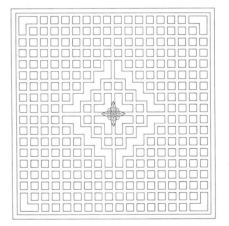

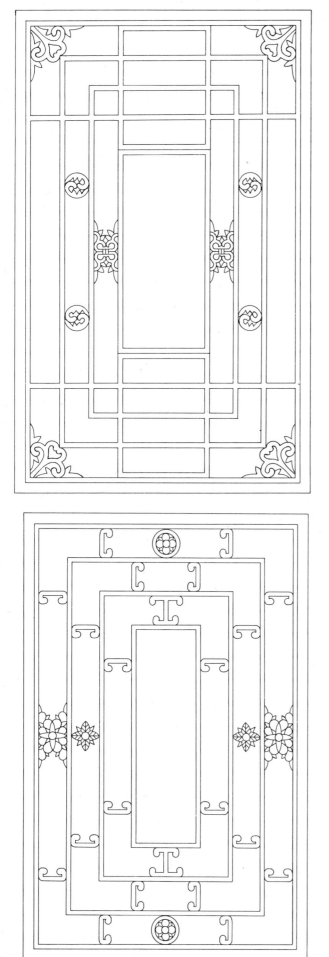

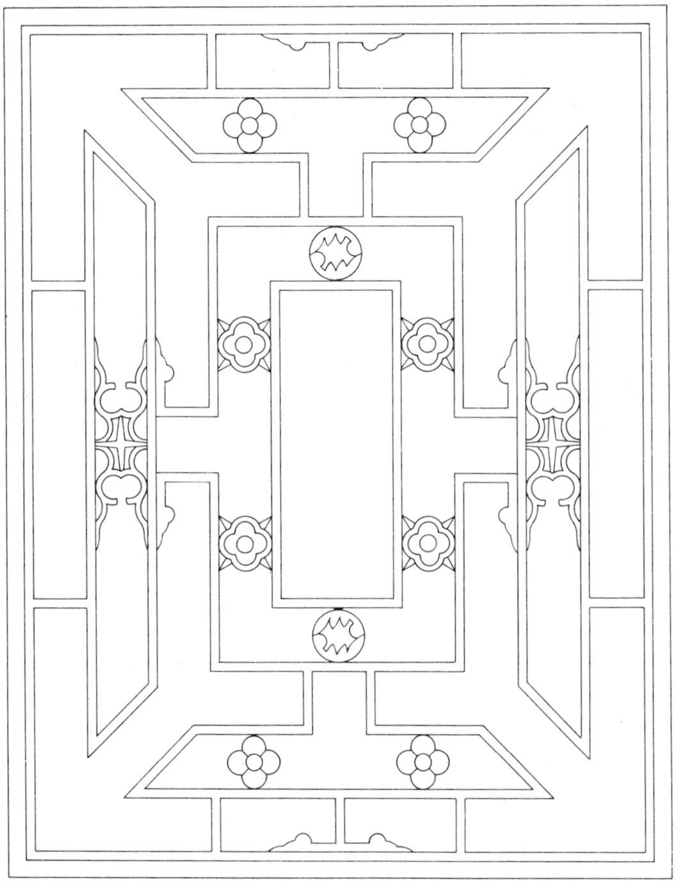

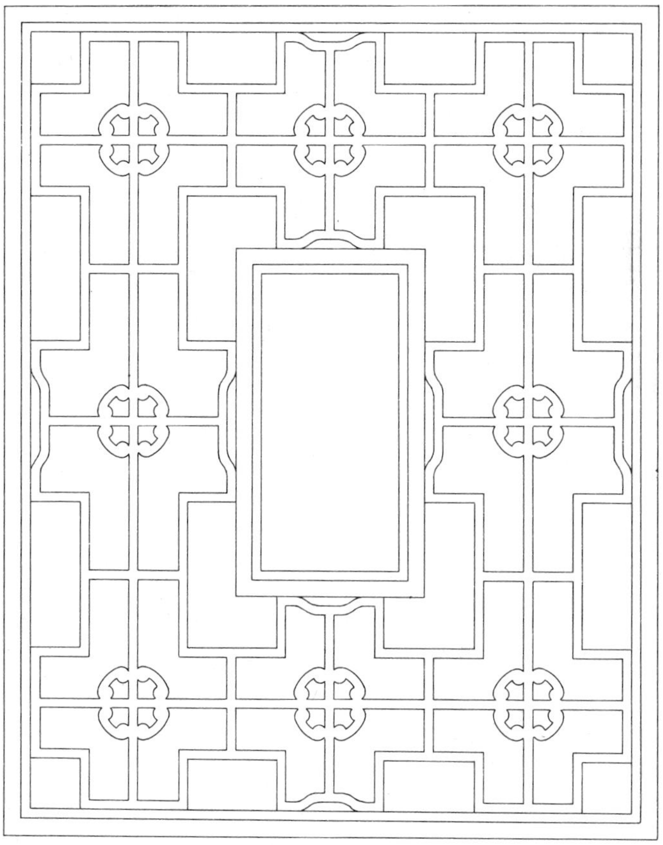

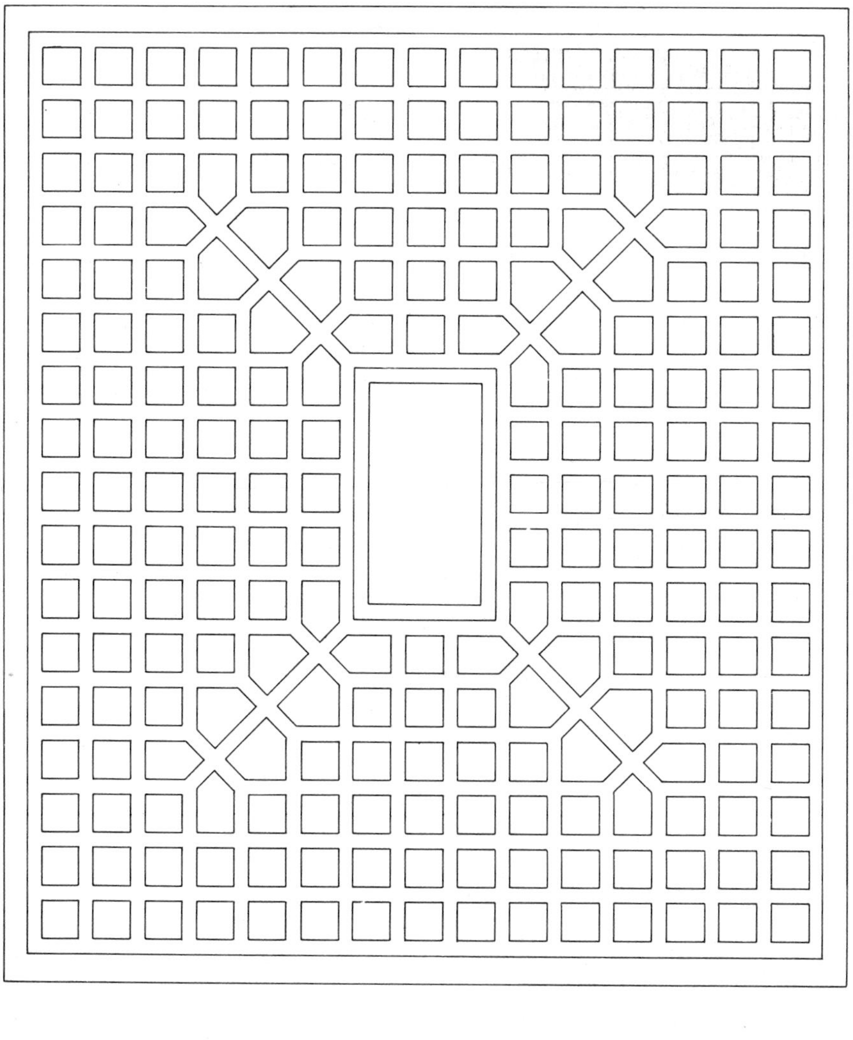

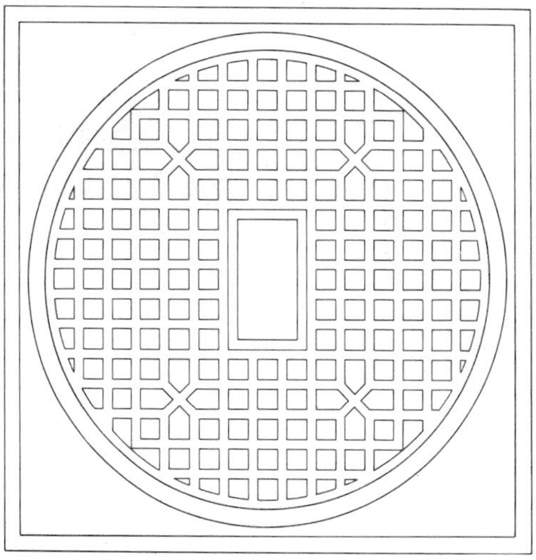

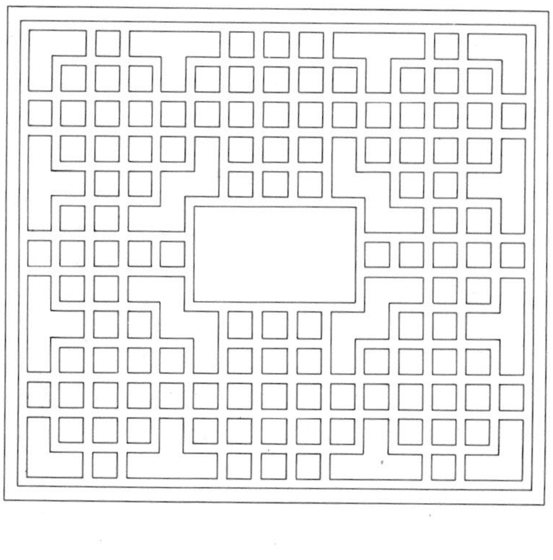

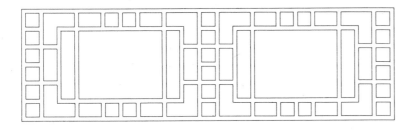

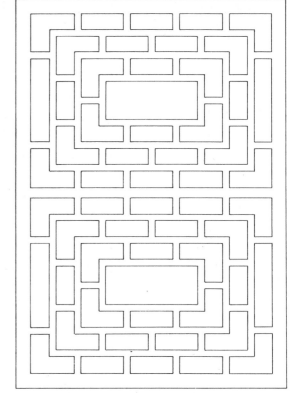

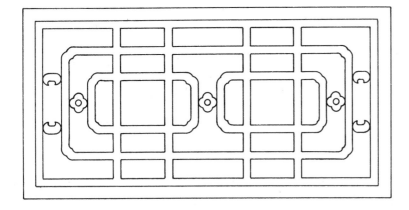

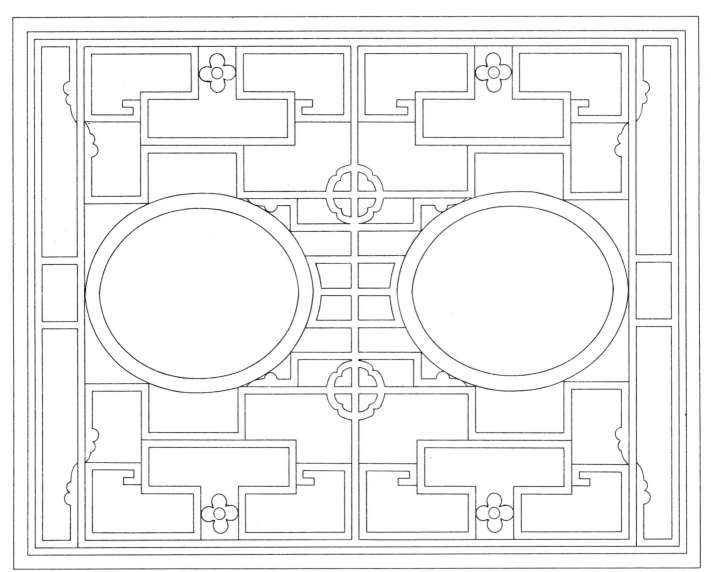

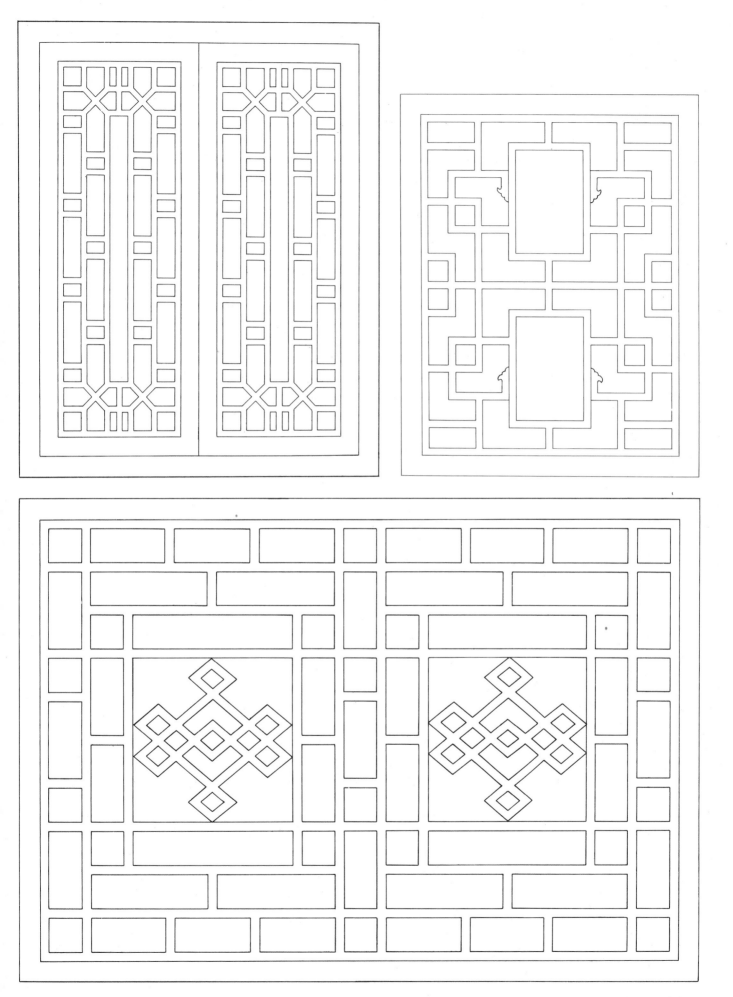

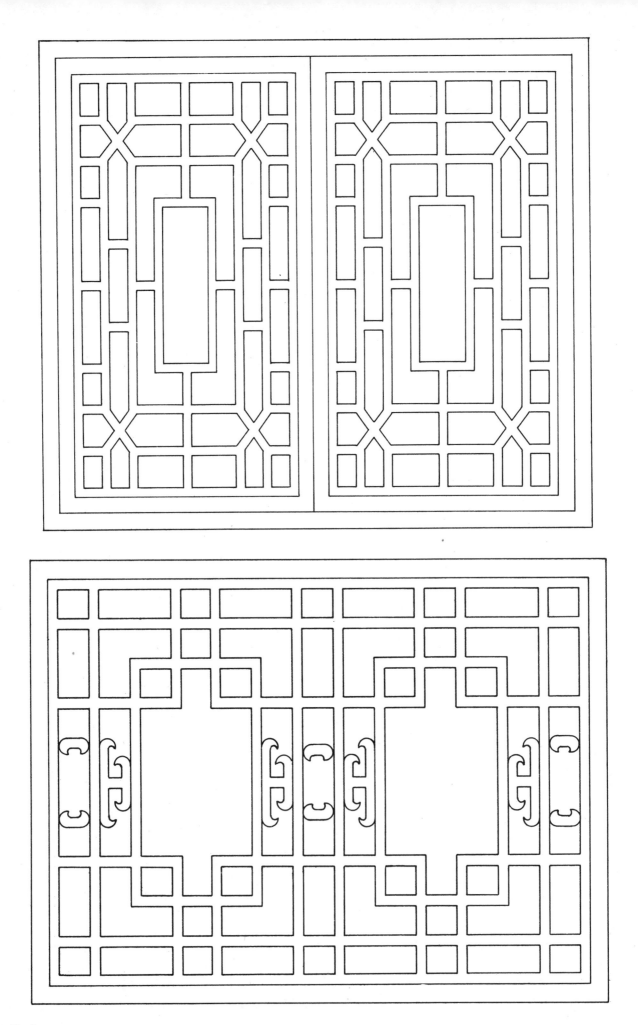

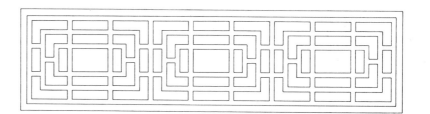

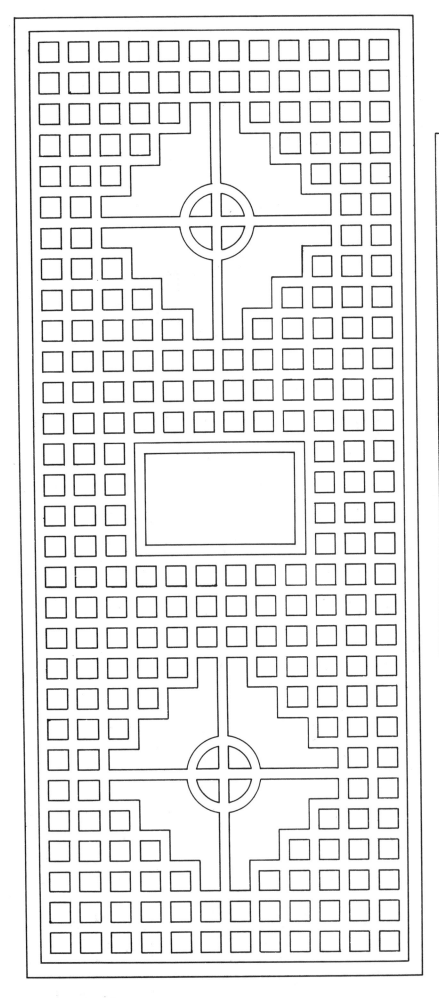

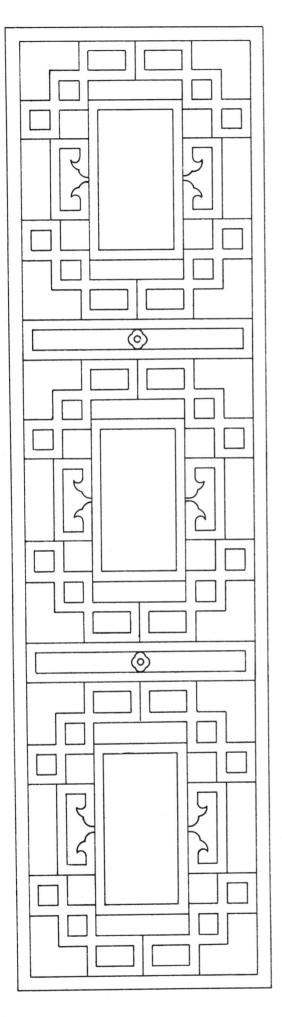

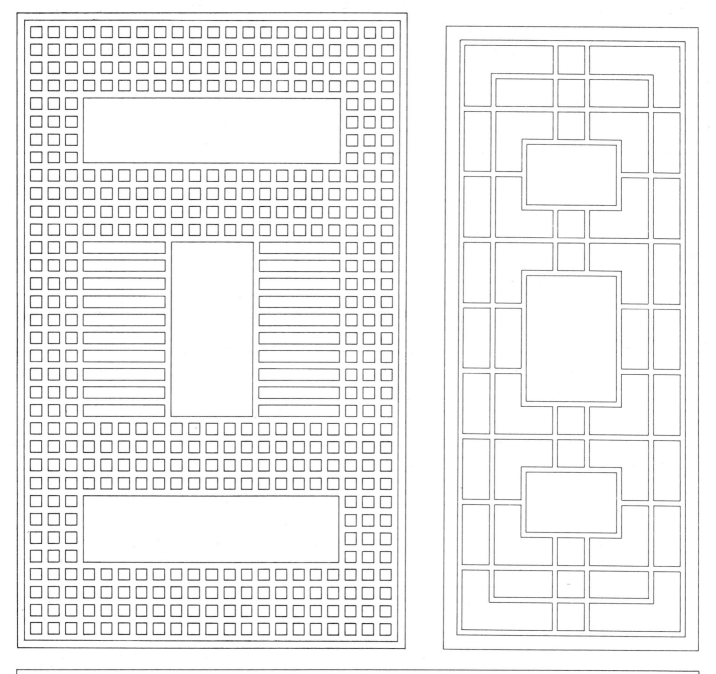

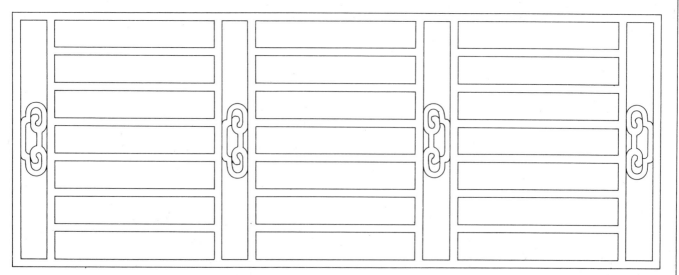

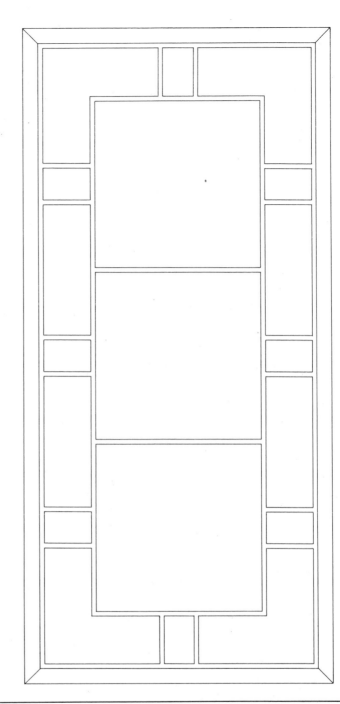
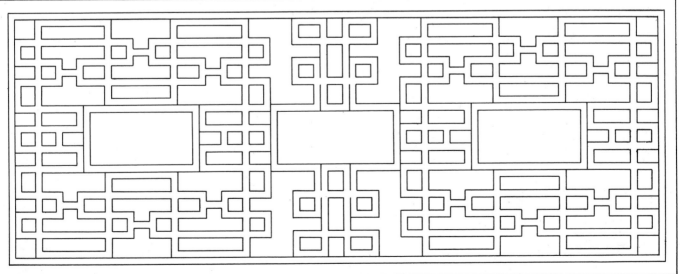

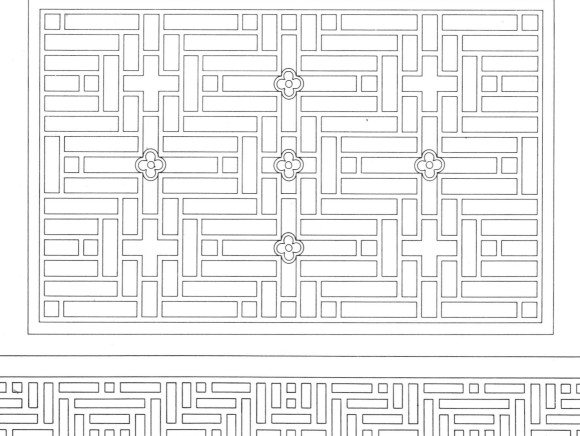

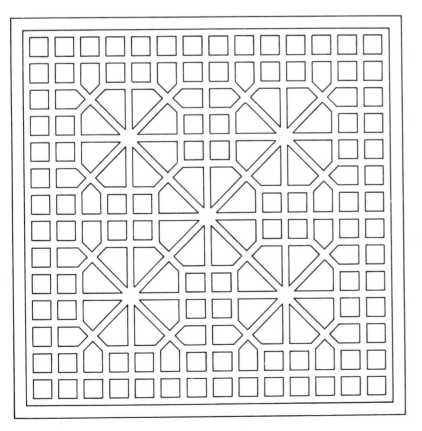

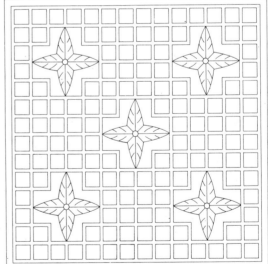

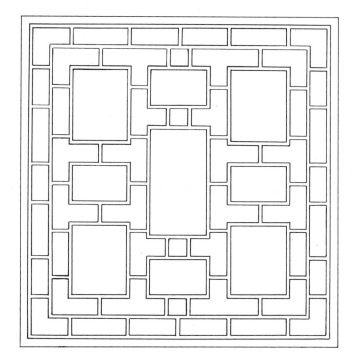

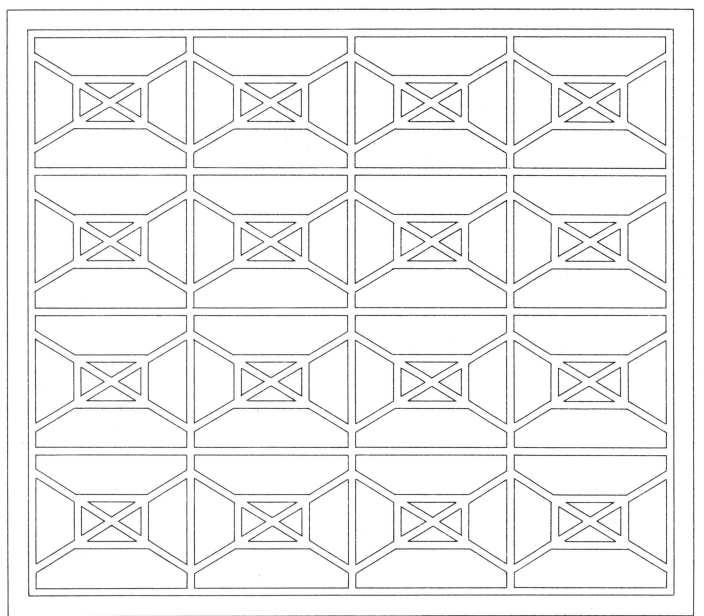

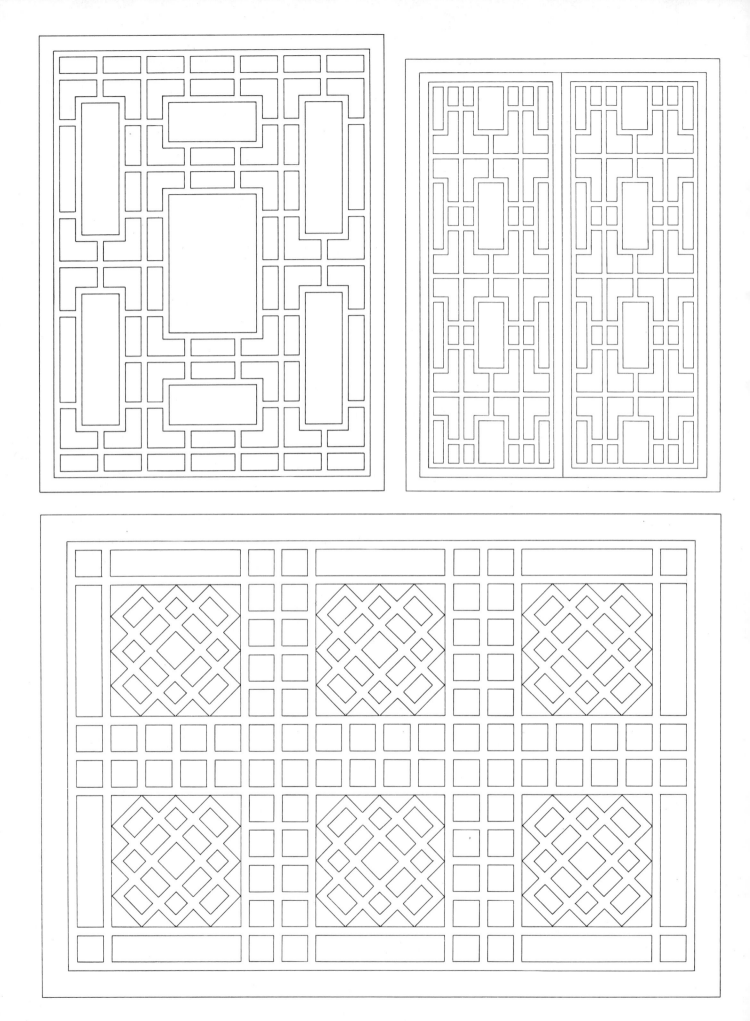

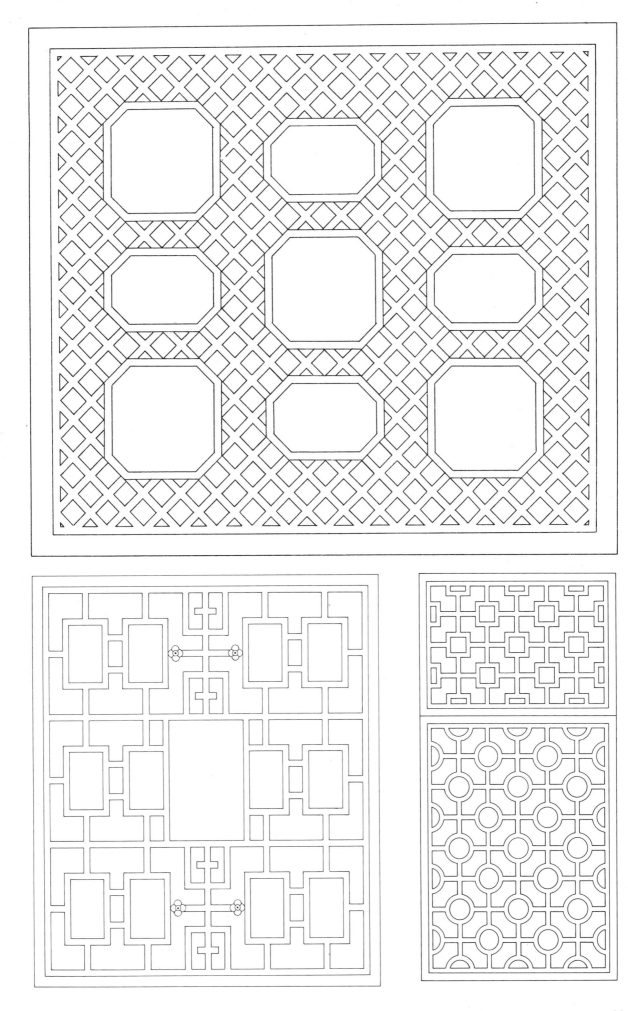

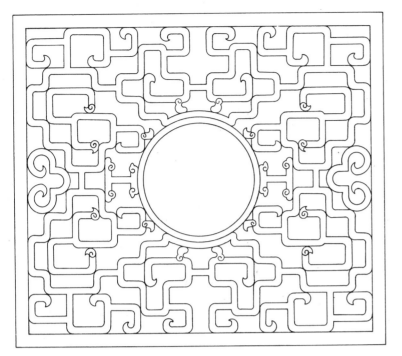

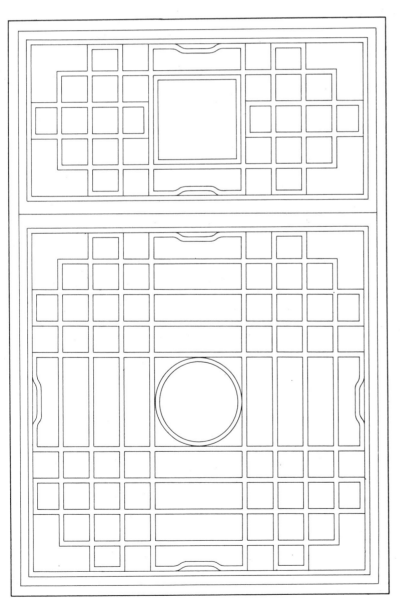

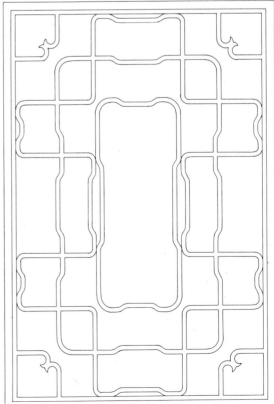

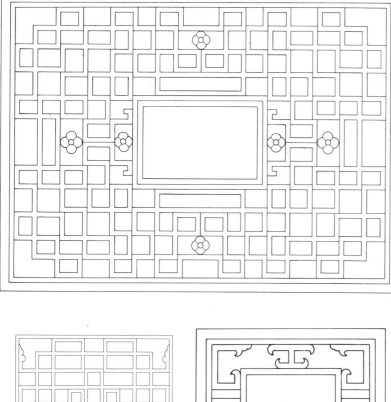

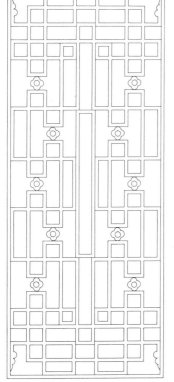

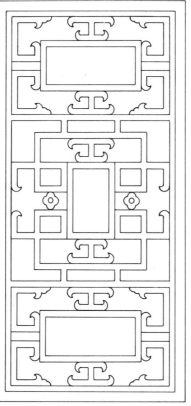

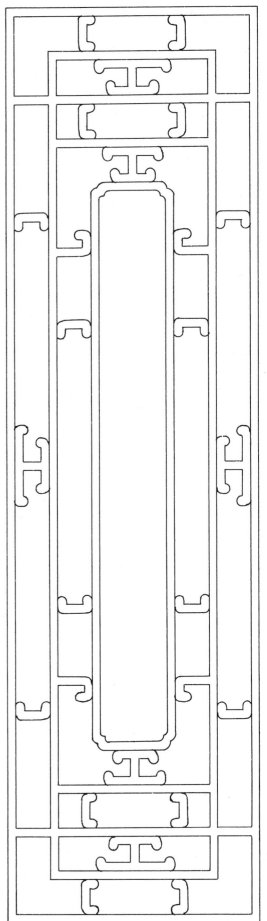

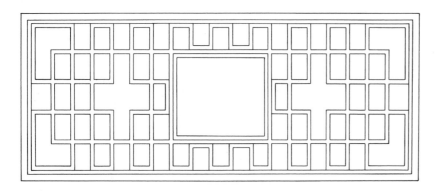

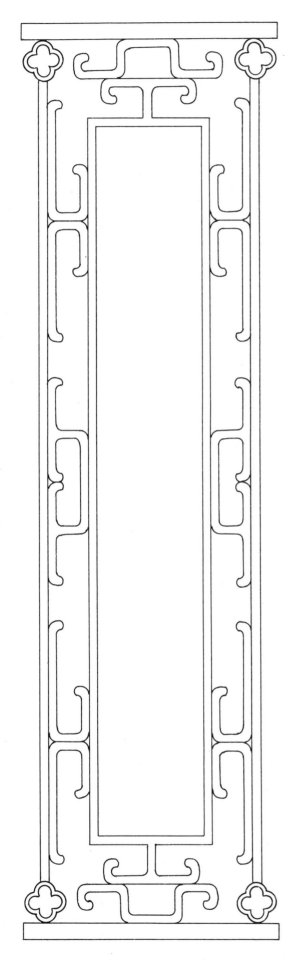

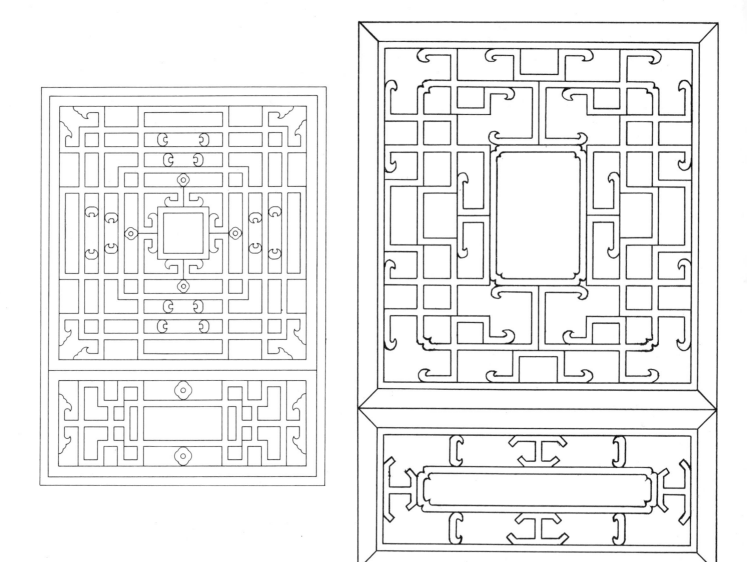
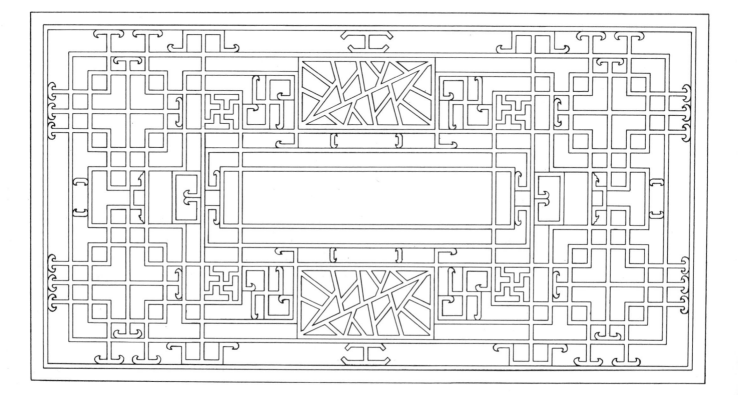

46   Wedge-Lock

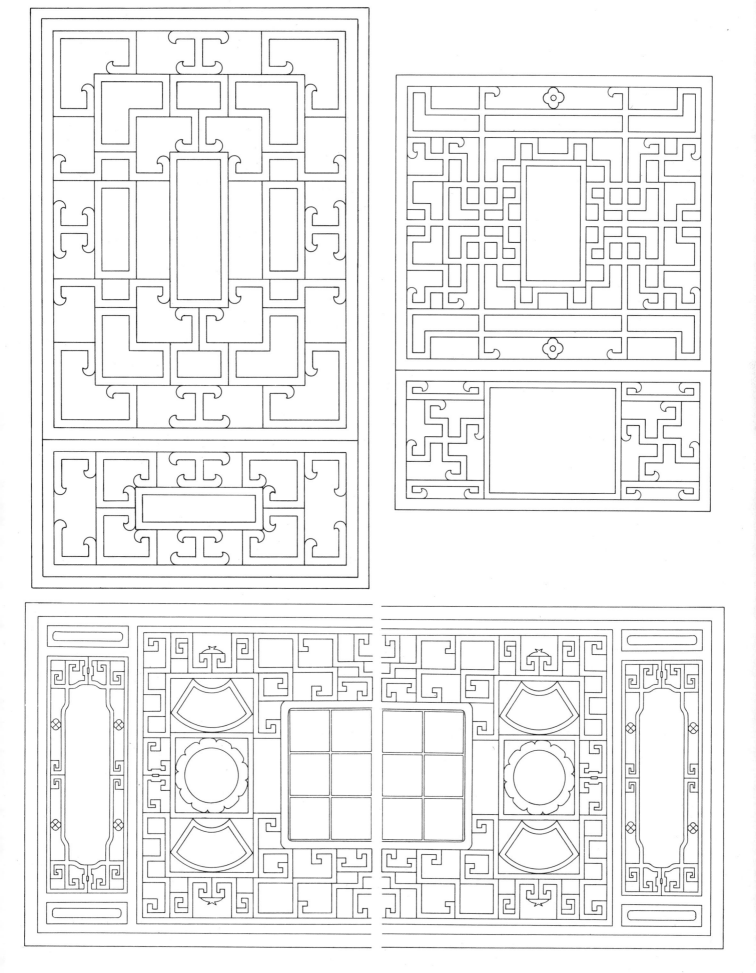

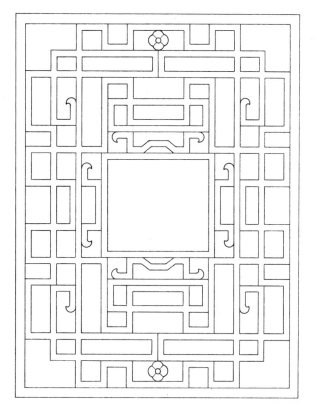

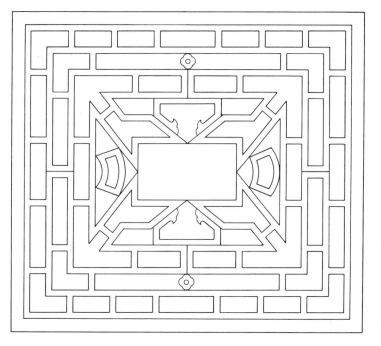

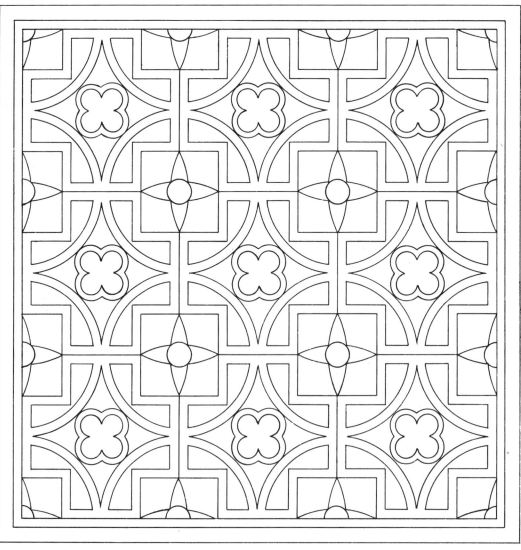

48   Wedge-Lock

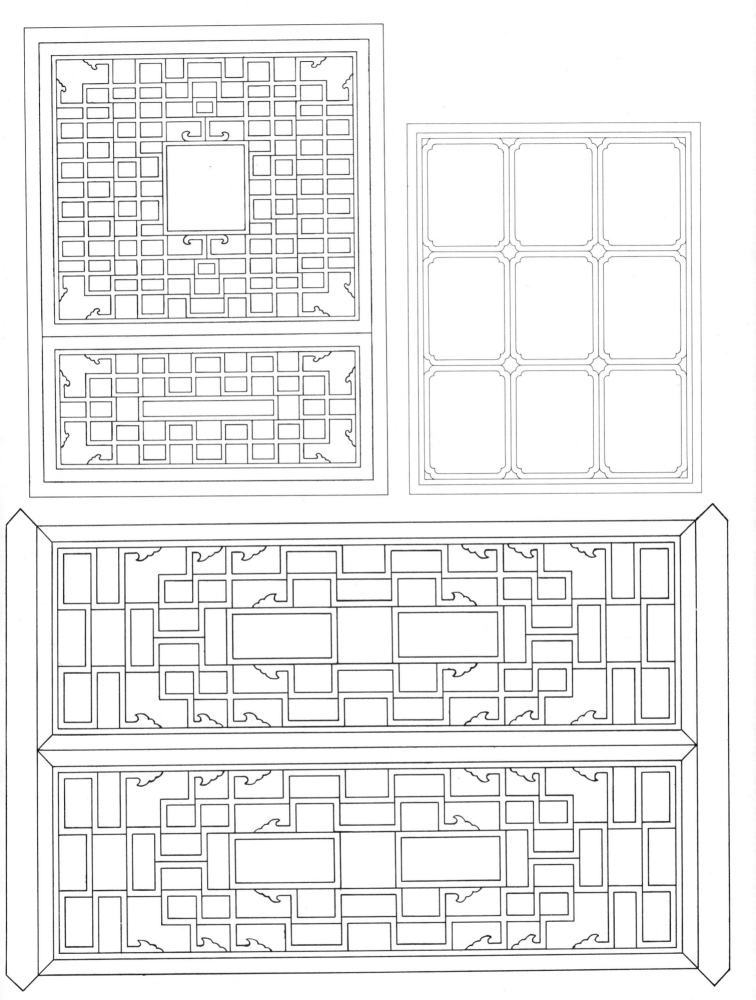

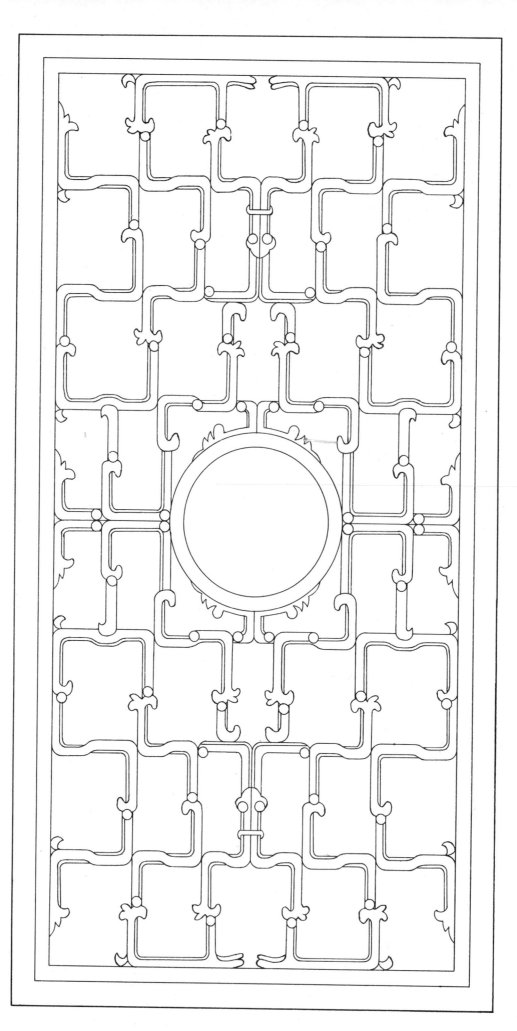

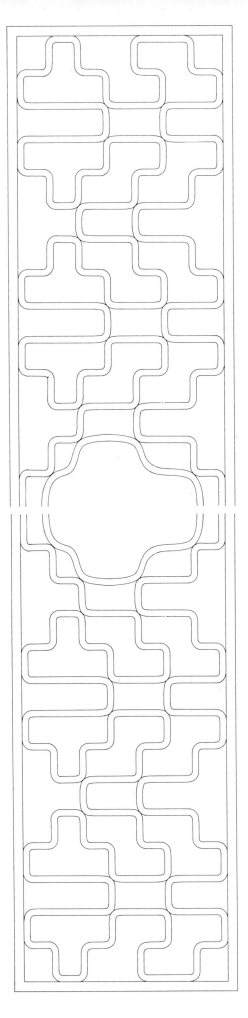

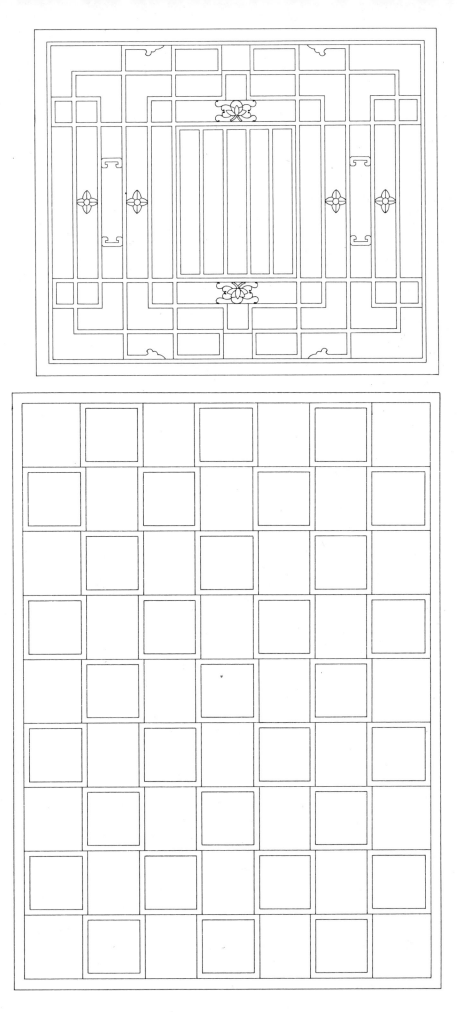

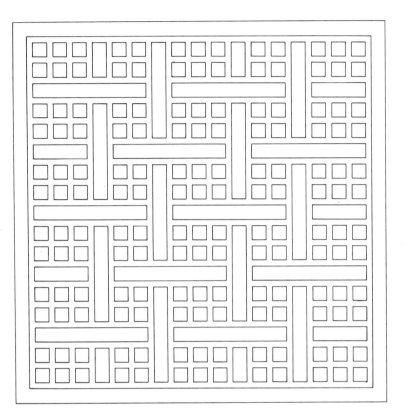

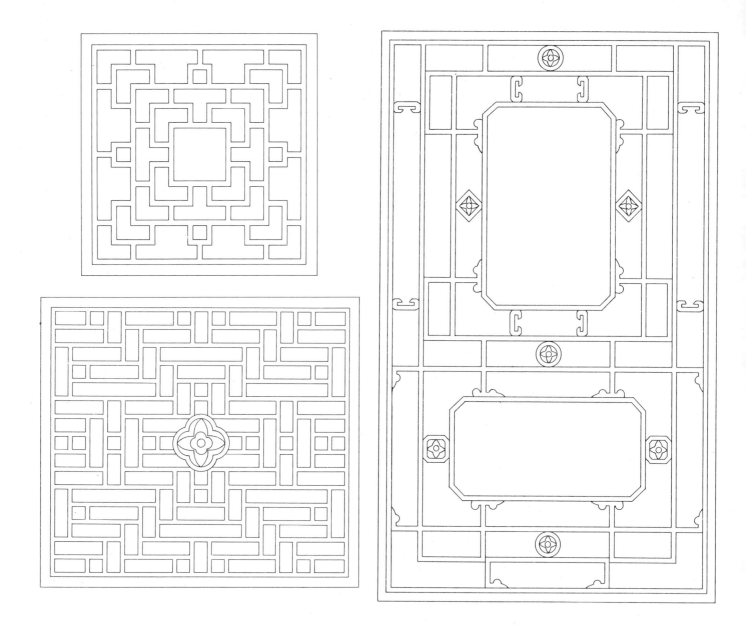

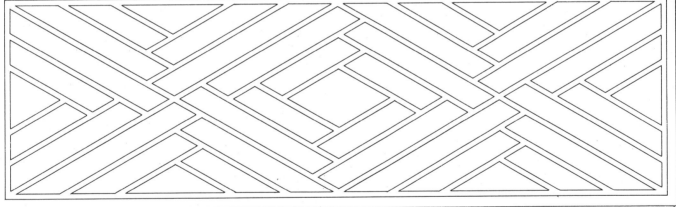

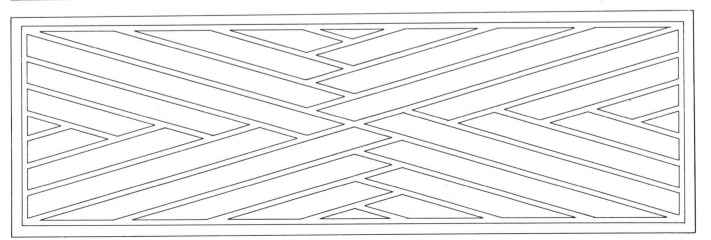

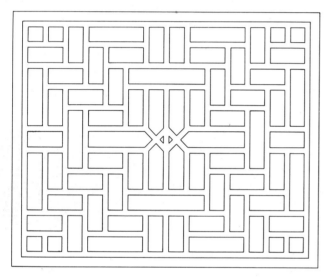

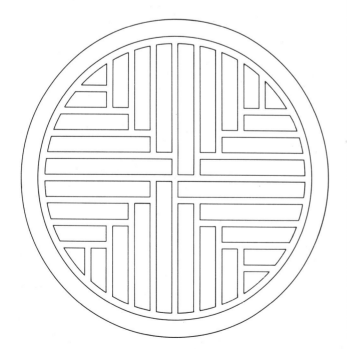

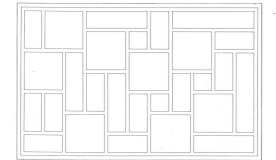

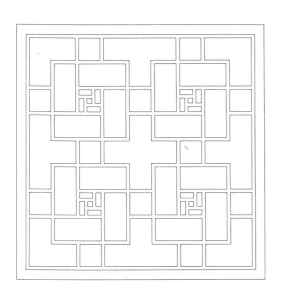

58   In-Out Bond

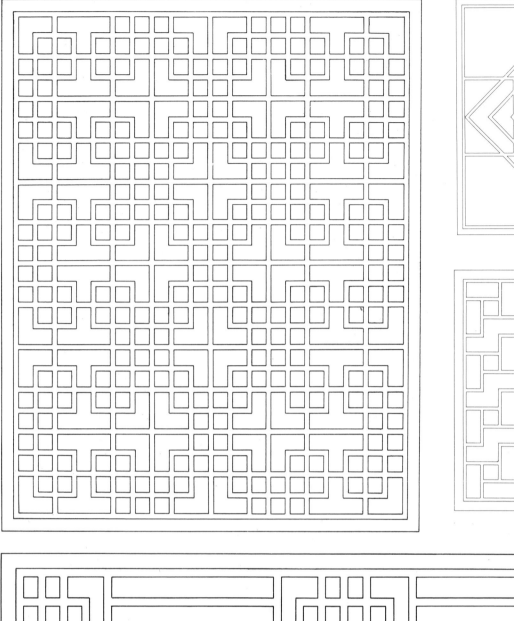

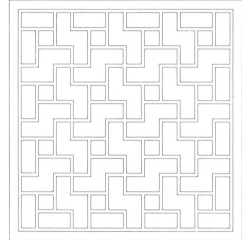

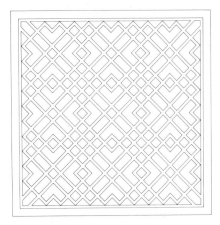

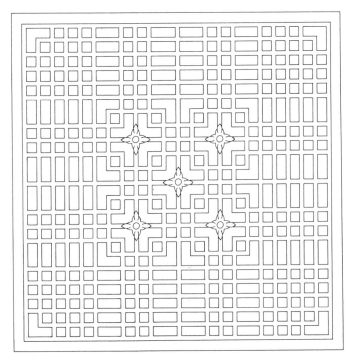

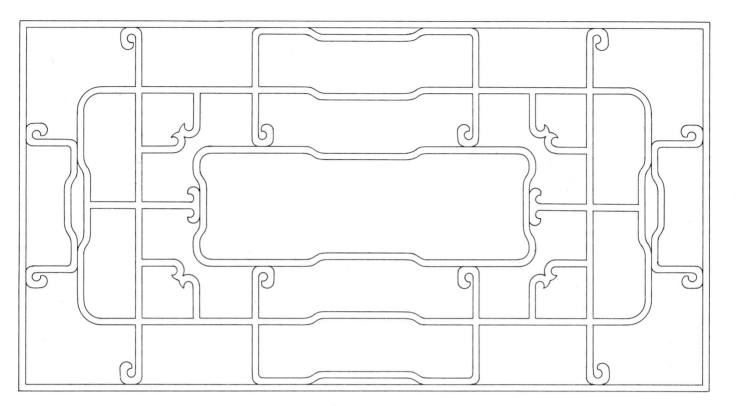

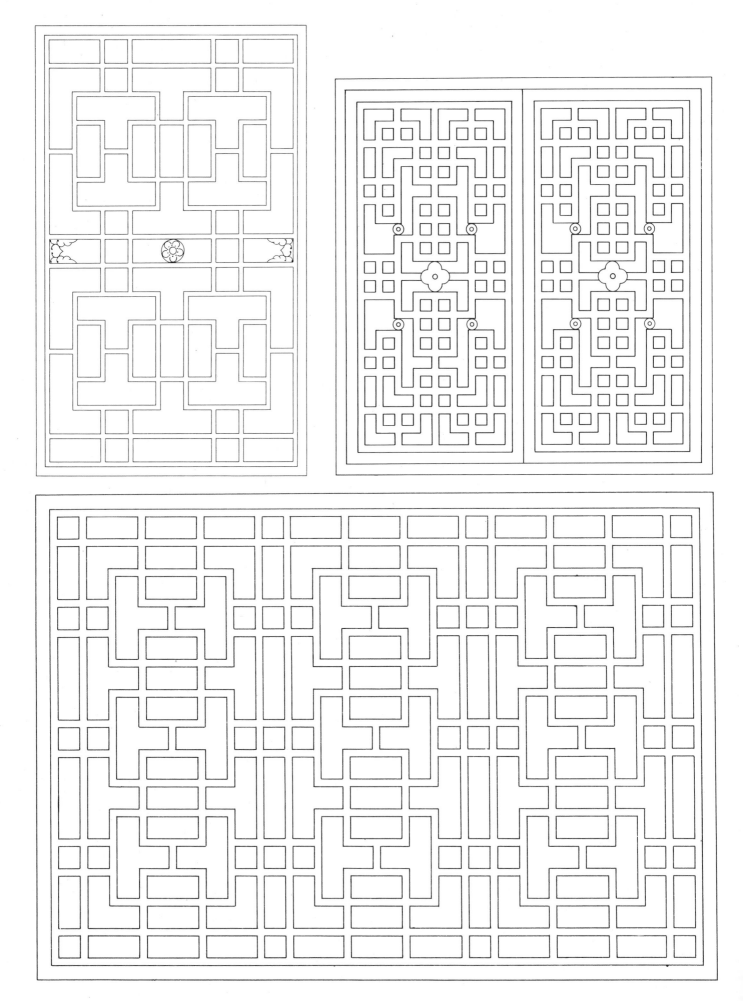

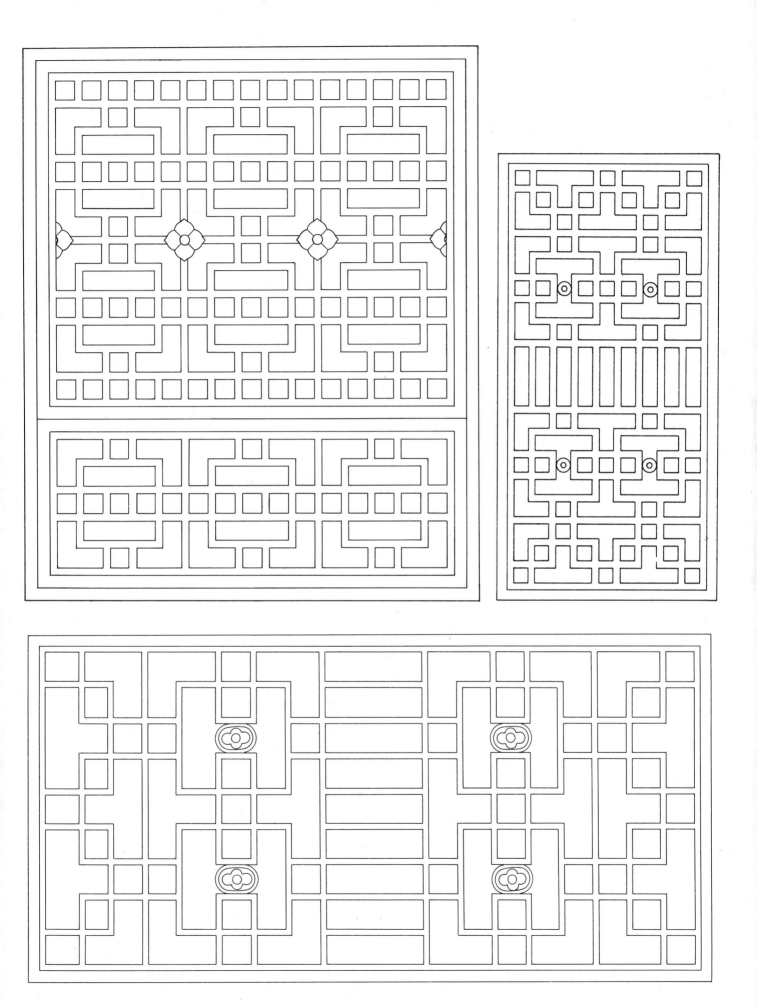

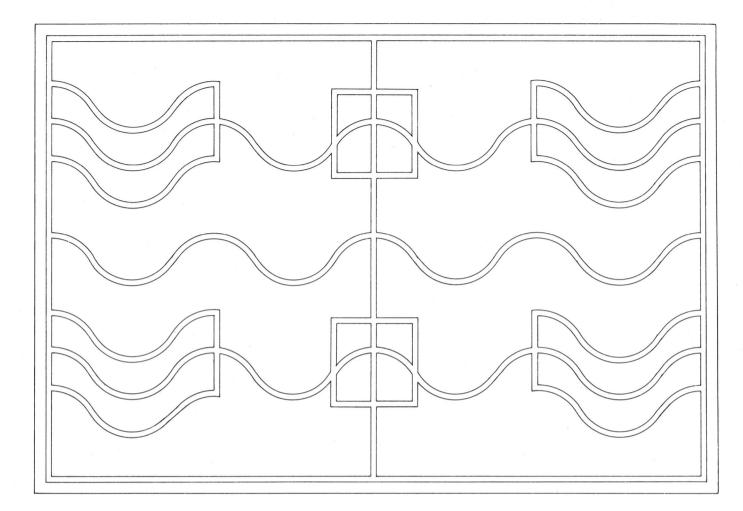

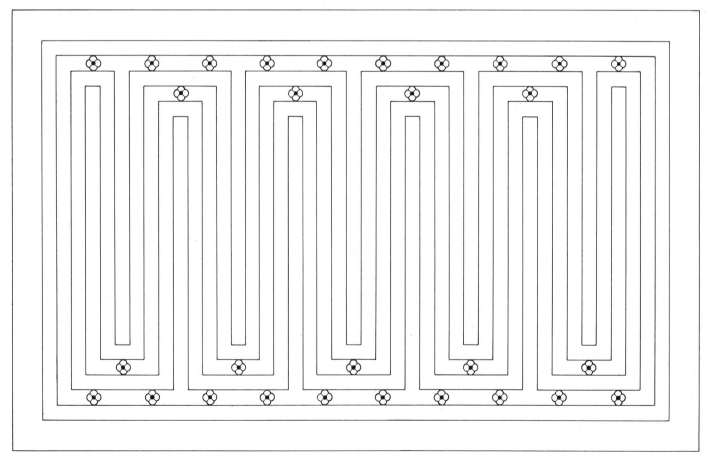

Parallel Waves 67

68   Opposed Waves

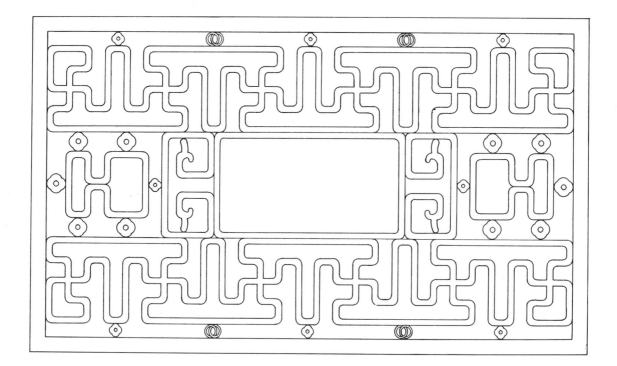

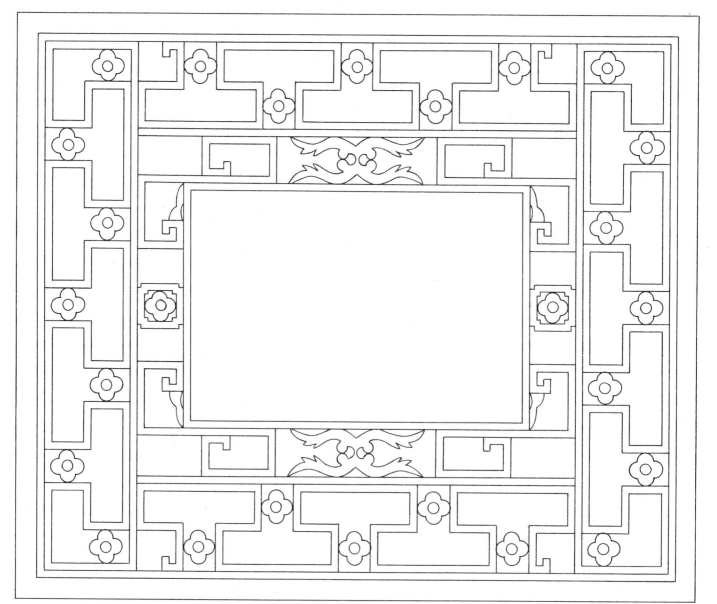

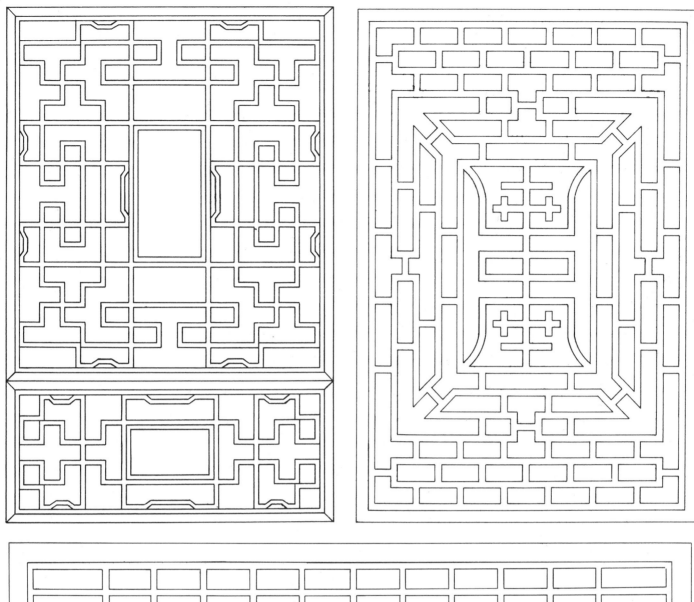

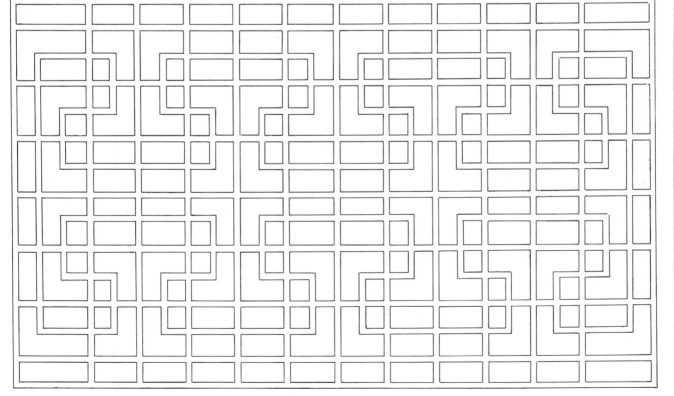

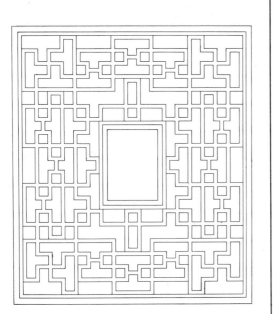

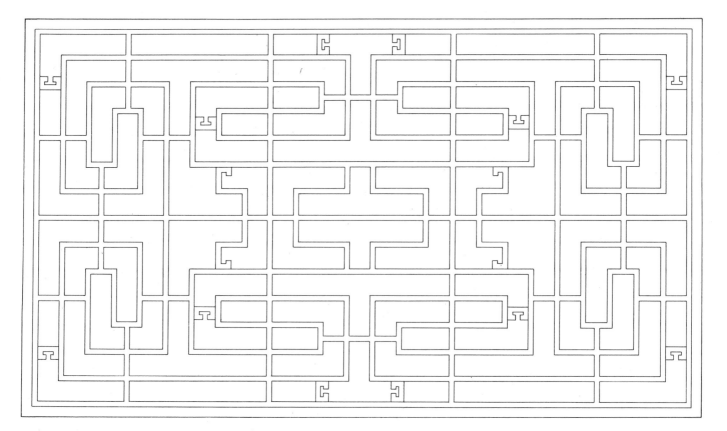

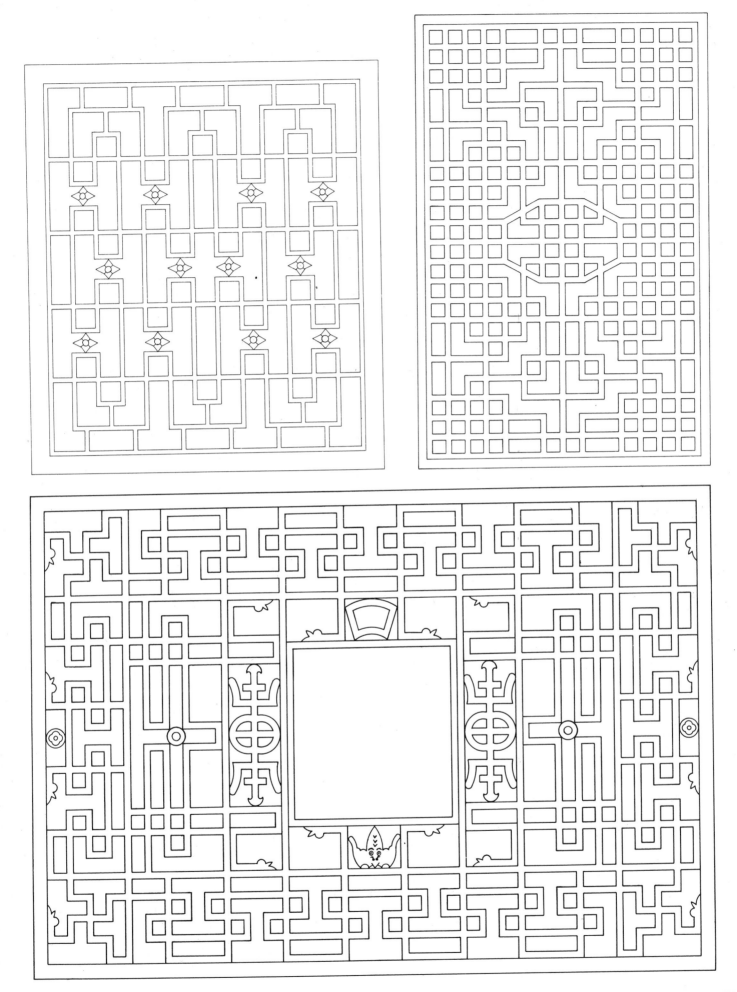

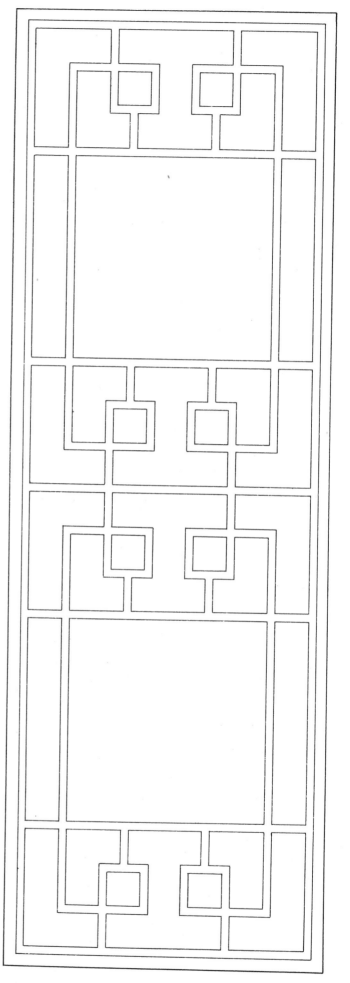

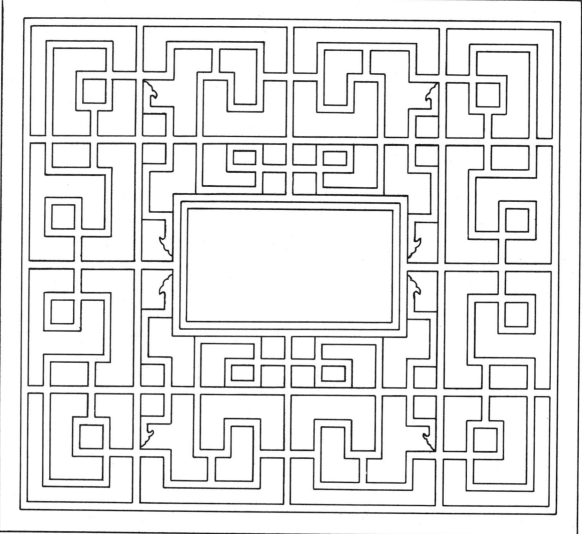

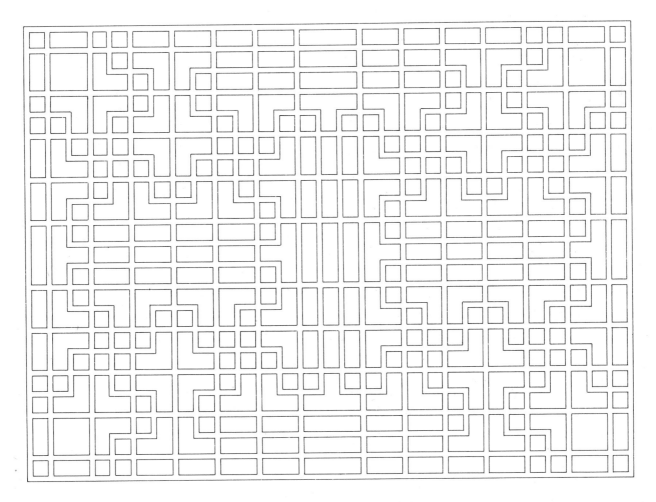

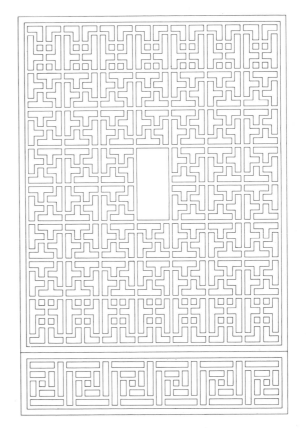

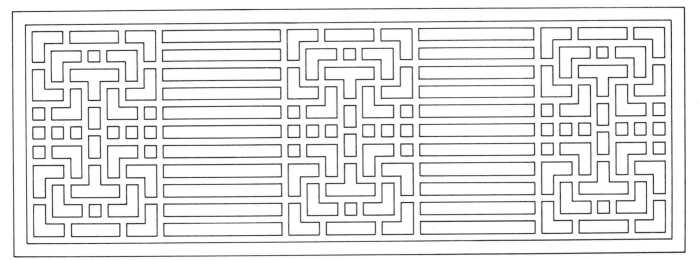

84   Allover Ju-I

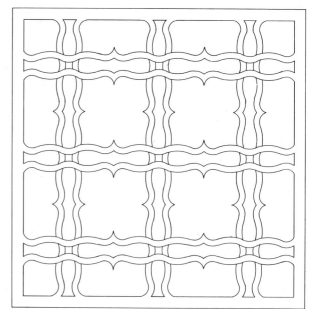

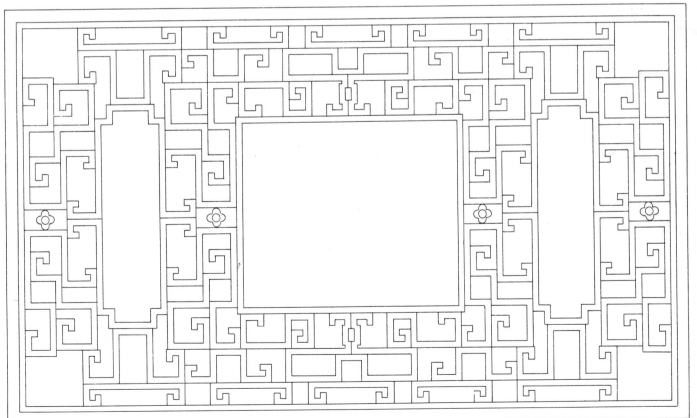

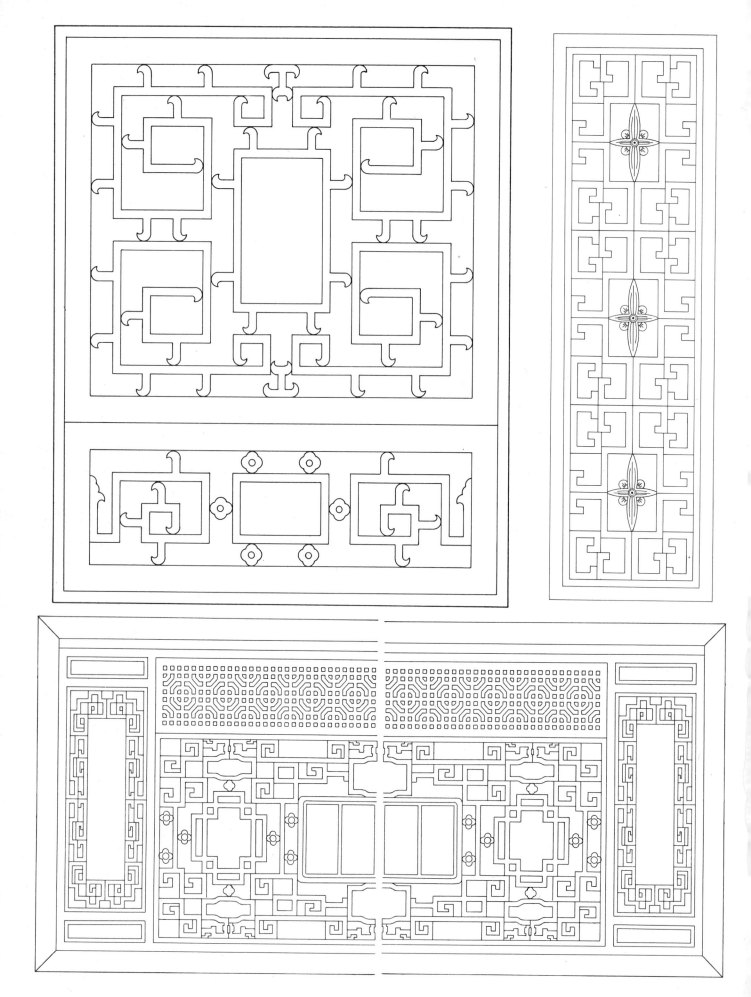

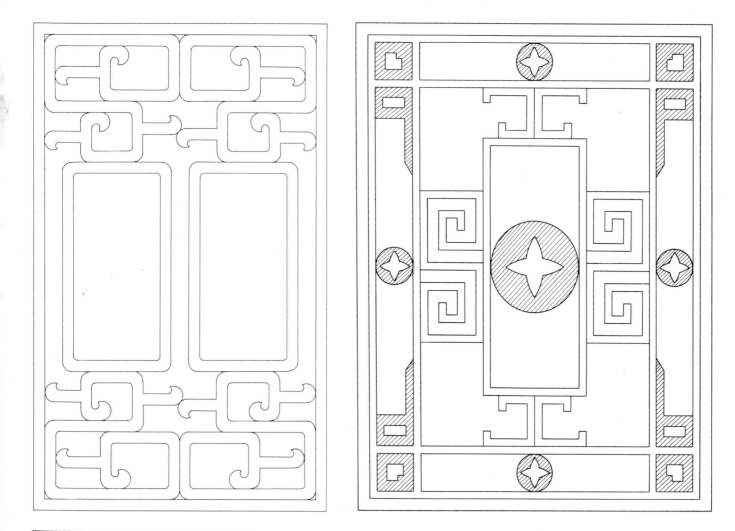

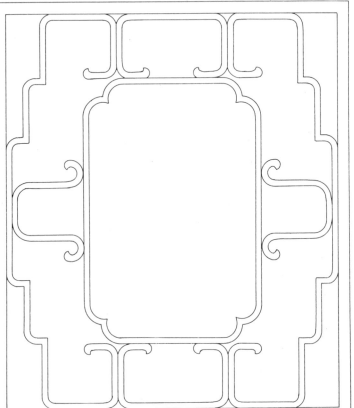

94   Rustic Ice-Ray

96   Rustic Ice-Ray

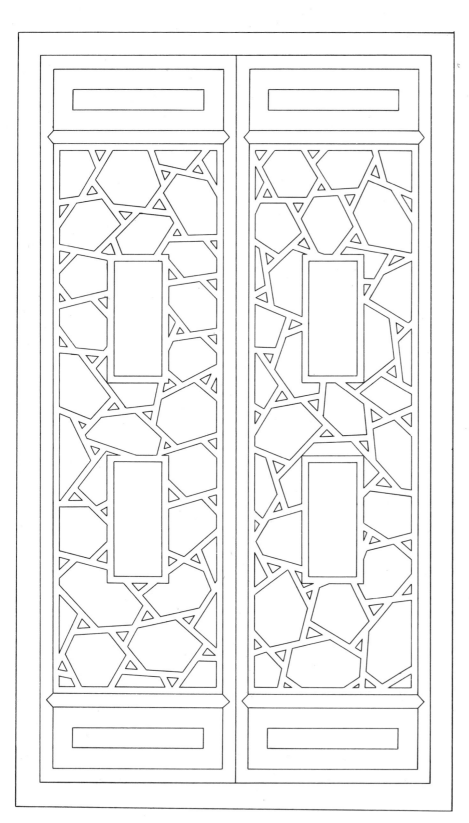

100 Symmetrical Ice-Ray

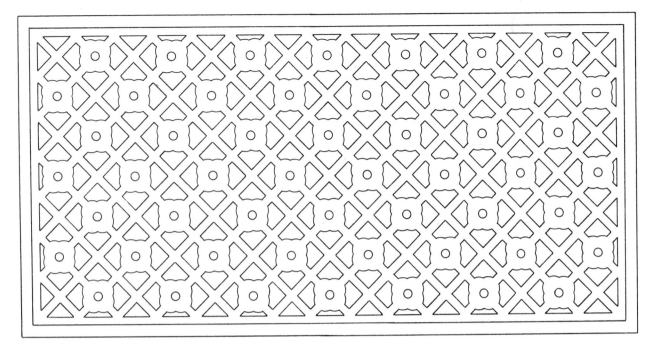

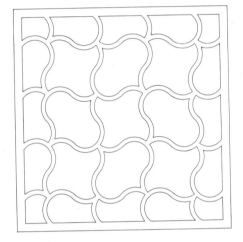

104   Square-Round

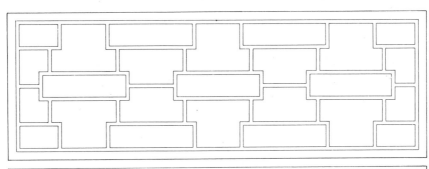

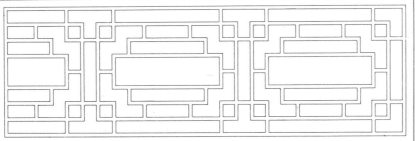

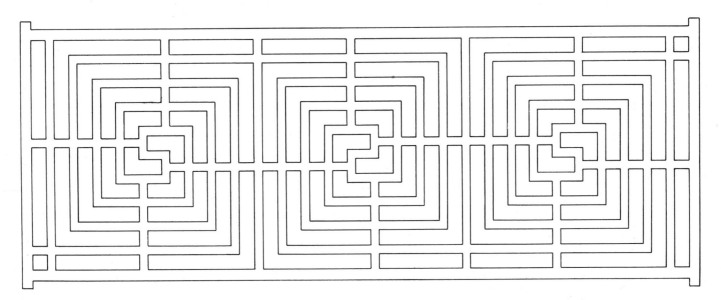

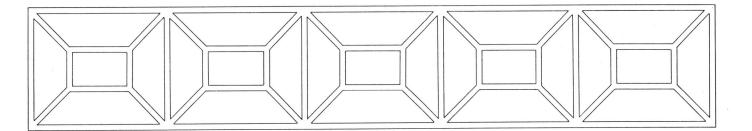

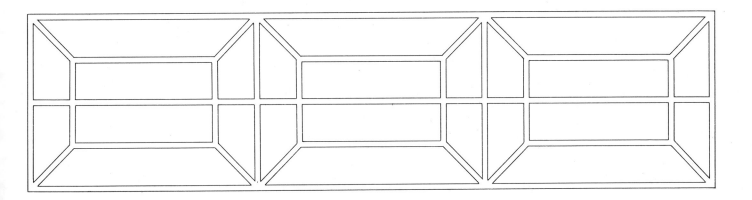

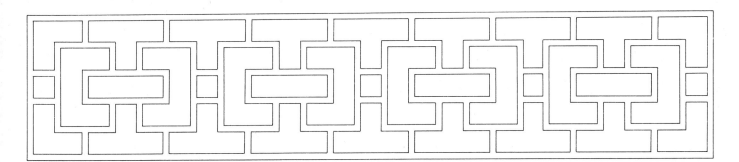

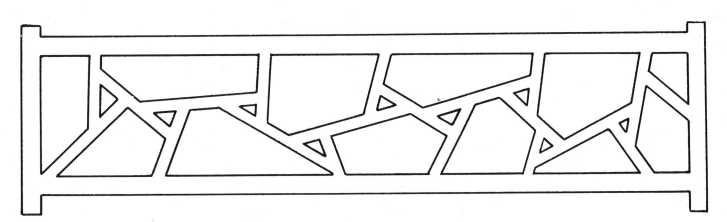

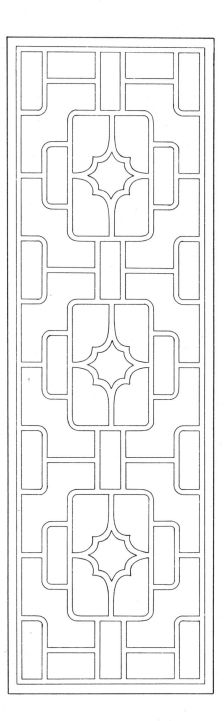

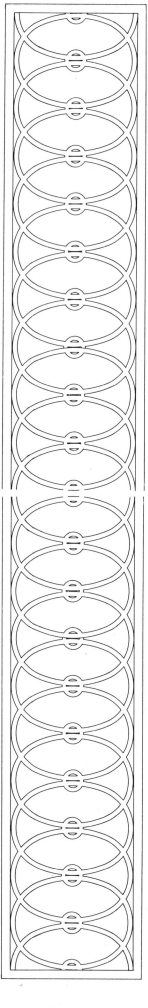

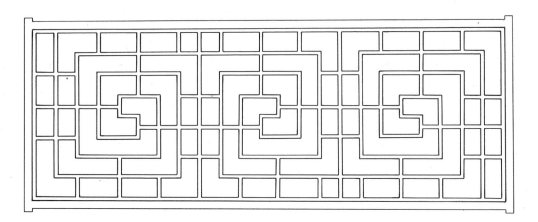

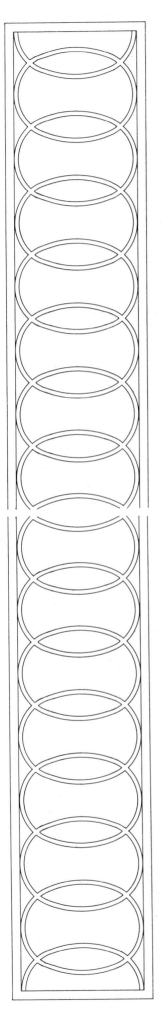

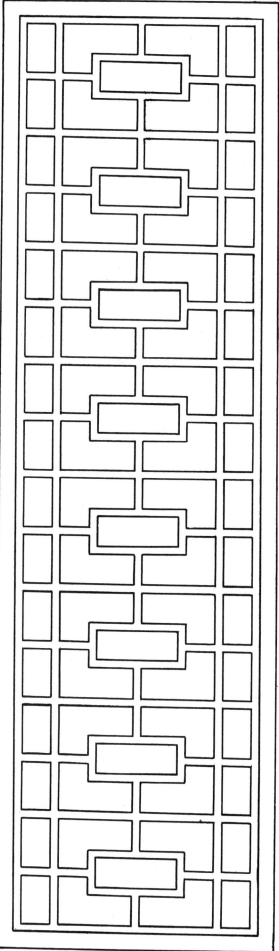

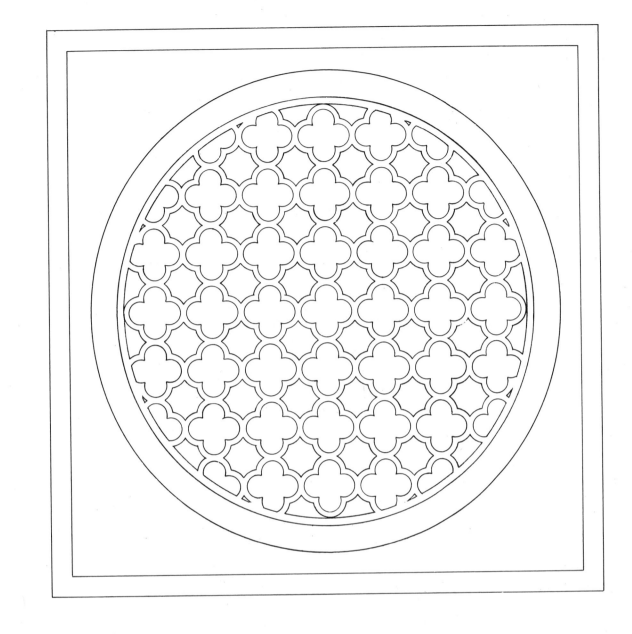

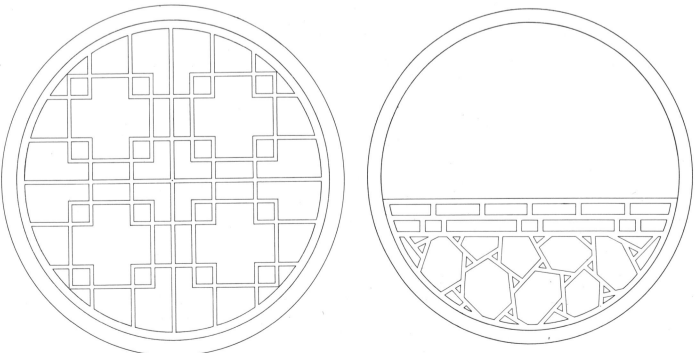

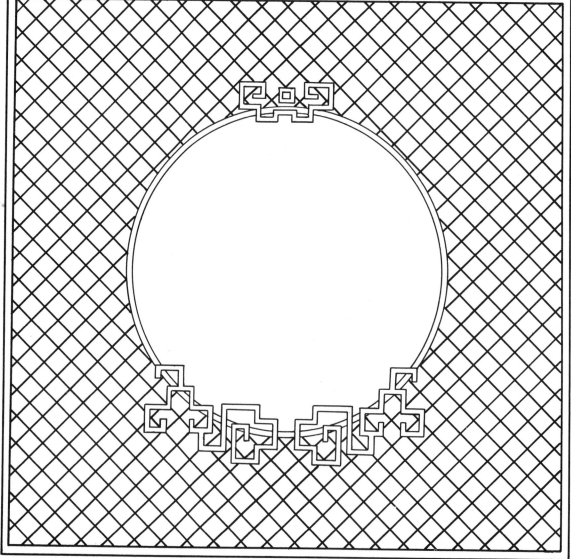

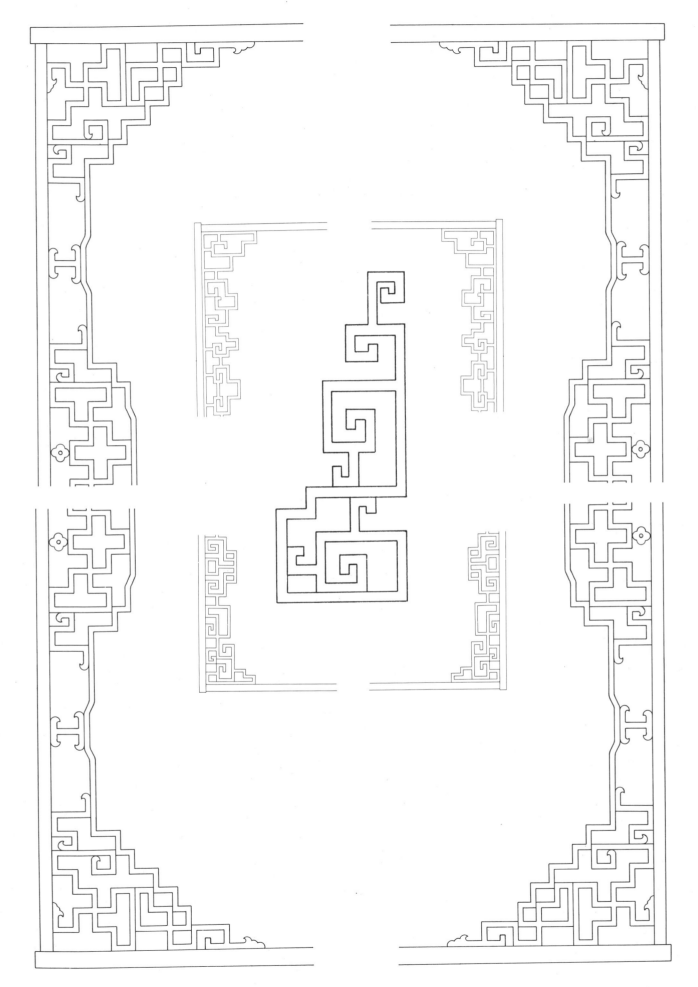